From The Women's Press Ltd
34 Great Sutton Street, London EC1V 0DX

Rukhsana Ahmad taught English Literature at the University of Karachi before moving to England where she now lives with her husband and three children. She works as a freelance writer and journalist.

She has written several plays, many of which have been produced in London and in the regions. Her most recent play, *Song for a Sanctuary*, toured Britain in June and October, 1991.

She was one of the founding members of the Asian Women Writers' Collective. Her short stories appear in *Right of Way* (The Women's Press, 1988), *The Inner Courtyard* (Virago, 1990) and *The Man Who Loved Presents* (The Women's Press, 1991).

Rukhsana Ahmad has also edited two community publications, *Dreams into Words* and *Daughters of the East* (Durham Voices, 1991), produced during a writing residency in Cleveland.

We Sinful Women

Contemporary Urdu Feminist Poetry
Translated and Edited by Rukhsana Ahmad

The Women's Press

Published in Great Britain by The Women's Press Ltd, 1991
A member of the Namara Group
34 Great Sutton Street, London EC1V 0DX.

Published in Pakistan, as *Beyond Belief*, by ASR Publications, Flat No. 8, 2nd Floor, Sheraz Plaza, Main Market, Gulberg II, P.O. Box 3154, Lahore, Pakistan, 1990.

Copyright © Rukhsana Ahmad, 1990
Copyright for the Urdu originals resides with the individual poets.

British Library Cataloguing in Publication Data
We sinful women: Urdu feminist poetry.
I. Ahmad, Rukhsana
891.43916

ISBN 0-7043-4262-6

The right of Rukhsana Ahmad to be identified as the author of this work has been asserted by her in accordance with the Copyright, Designs and Patents Act, 1988.

The Women's Press and Rukhsana Ahmad thank the Arts Council Translation Fund for donating a grant for the publication of *We Sinful Women*.

Typeset by Contour Typesetters, Southall, London
Printed and bound in Great Britain by
Cox & Wyman, Reading, Berkshire

To My Mother

CONTENTS

Introduction
Rukhsana Ahmad

Kishwar Naheed

We Sinful Women	31
Section 144	35
A Palace of Wax	37
The Grass Is Really Like Me	41
Who Am I?	43
Nightmare	47
Censorship	51
Talking to Myself	55
Anticlockwise	59
To the Masters of Countries with a Cold Climate	63

Fahmida Riaz

Stoning	67
Surah I Yaaseen	69
O God of Heaven and Earth	71
Come, Give Me Your Hand	73
To Auden	77
Virgin	79
The Interrogator	81
Image	85
Search Warrant	87
Chadur and Diwari	91
She Is a Women Impure	97
Akleema	99
The Laughter of a Woman	101

Sara Shagufta

Woman and Salt	103

To Daughter, Sheely	107
The Moon Is Quite Alone	109

Zehra Nigah

Compromise	113
The Moonflower Tree	115
My Crime: A Promise	119
The Girl by the Lamp-Post	125
My Playmate	131
Hudood Ordinance	137

Ishrat Aafreen

Dedication	141
I	143
Introduction	145
Migration	147
Dialogue with an Incomplete Man	149
The First Prayer of My Elders	151
Liberation	155
Ghazal	159
Ghazal	161
Ghazal	163
Ghazal	165
Ghazal	167
Ghazal	169
The Daughter of Riches	173

Saeeda Gazdar

Twelfth of February, 1983	177

Neelma Sarwar

The Thief	187
Prison	189
To the First Man to Be Awarded Lashes	191
I Wish That Day of Judgment Would Come	193

INTRODUCTION

For a long time Urdu poetry has been dominated by male figures whose reputations, established and confirmed by male critics, remain colossal in comparison with those of the women poets. Many of the poets represented in this volume are established and well known in Pakistan, but the literary establishment always implies that women poets are a special case: they achieve publication and, sometimes, celebrity, because they are women rather than because they are poets. This is essentially not unlike the patronising recognition which is awarded to women's and black writers' achievements in the West. They are easily marginalised by the implication that the interest in the work derives from its rarity rather than from any intrinsic qualities the work itself might possess. The source of the prejudice in both cases is exactly the same: the conservatism of literary establishments and their stranglehold on aesthetic values, their tendency to dismiss work to which they cannot themselves relate and their inability to empathise with work that derives directly from women's experiences.

In a male-dominated society devoted to the past, it is not surprising that the most popular women poets would be those who conform to both socio-cultural and literary traditions. Yet the women poets who attracted my interest, and whose work I have found the most exciting, represent brave departures from that literary tradition.

Traditional Urdu Poetry

Urdu is one of the relatively young languages from the subcontinent. It grew as a *lingua franca* for the troops in India, soon after the Muslim invasions of the subcontinent, between the twelfth and fourteenth centuries. As a hybrid deriving from quite different languages: Persian, Arabic and the native North Indian dialects, Urdu combined contrasting qualities and offered enormous flexibility. But it remained somewhat derided and did not acquire a literature until much later. Persian, the language of the courts, used for formal communications and for literary expression, was the language of the élite. Classical Persian literature exercised tremendous influence on Urdu poetry when it began to develop, around the seventeenth century, an influence that remained strong until quite recently.

Curiously enough, Urdu poetry has a stronger tradition behind it than Urdu prose. It flourished in cities like Delhi, Lucknow and Hyderabad, rapidly attaining its zenith in Mughal times under the patronage of rich Muslim rulers who often employed poets. In return, poets were expected to pay homage to their patrons and to deliver poems to mark important occasions. The most highly regarded and popular Urdu poet, Mirza Asadullah Khan Ghalib, lived in the shadows of the dying Mughal court of Bahadur Shah Zafar in the first half of the nineteenth century. It was, overwhelmingly, a man's world. The images of women that Urdu poetry offered were not unlike those glimpsed in Elizabethan sonnets: the love that it celebrated was, likewise, often unrequited. A feckless beloved, endowed with heavenly beauty, reigned: fair of face, doe-eyed, dark-haired, tall and willowy, a woman who vacillated from indifference, shyness and modesty to wanton wilfulness and cruelty. For her the poet was willing to die. It was a stylised and charming tradition but it was also hidebound in its strictures, formalism and usage.

Though there had been some mild expressions of social consciousness and comment in the nineteenth century, Urdu poetry was, primarily, romantic and idealised. It was the poet Iqbal, in the 1930s, who really established political themes as valid subject matter. In the forties, the Progressive Writers' Association forged ahead and revived Urdu literature with the energy of the freedom movement that was vibrating through India. Urdu fiction triumphed in the work of successful but controversial writers such as Saadat Hasan Manto and Ismat Chughtai, one of the major women writers from the subcontinent. A collection of short stories, *Angaarey*, was banned by the British because of fears that it might cause unrest. The work of Ali Sardar Jafri, Mukhdoom, Meeraji and, later, N M Rashid and Faiz Ahmad Faiz added to the depth and richness of which the language was capable, laying the foundations of contemporary Urdu literature. However, with the exception of Meeraji and N M Rashid, most of the new generation of poets challenged content rather than the established forms.

The *ghazal*, which is still the most popular conventional form, can be set to music. It requires an ornamental style of writing and has a definable register for this purpose. In common with the sonnet it has a structured rhyme scheme and carefully controlled rhythm. Traditionally, it begins with a rhymed couplet. Each following couplet introduces a new idea linked to the central theme largely by the rhyme established at the outset. The closing couplet is also rhymed and may introduce the name of the poet. Conceits and exaggeration come naturally to the *ghazal* writer.

The bulk of published Urdu poetry still tends to be love poetry bound in the old idioms and conceits. It is not surprising, then, that when women wanted to use the medium to convey real, contemporary issues they had to abandon the more conventional forms, with their traditional images of women, and had to look at the possibilities of extending the language. Poems like 'Censorship', 'Section 144', 'Search Warrant' and 'Twelfth of February, 1983' are not only deliberately political, they are also consciously averse to the stilted, formal diction popular with earlier

Urdu poets. Poems like 'Virgin', 'She Is a Woman Impure', 'Who Am I?' 'Woman and Salt' and 'Dialogue with an Incomplete Man' not only refuse to conform to the notion of the ideal woman, they set out to defy it and to claim a new identity.

Fahmida Riaz has given the most thought to the issue of language and its links with working people. She deliberately chooses words which are rustic and/or of Indic origin instead of their literary, Persianised equivalents, always preferred by earlier poets, which are, naturally, less accessible to the masses and tend to make poetry more élitist. The 'political' attempts to move Urdu in the direction of Persian and Arabic by the Pakistani government and to Sanskritise Hindi by the Indian government, have had the effect of drawing those two mutually intelligible languages and their users apart. There is, she claims, no need for language to reflect religious ancestry and connections in any way. She finds greater vitality in the language of peasants and working people as it is less remote from reality than classical Persian and is constantly sustained by it.

Kishwar Naheed, who began her literary career writing in traditional forms, confesses that, increasingly, she finds them restrictive for the expression of any radical thought. There is a loftiness of style, which is so ingrained into the *ghazal* form, that lines such as:

> Let me dry my wet clothes in these courtyards . . .

or:

> for every morning I am slaughtered at my office desk,
> for telling lies . . .

would be hopelessly out of place in it. Perhaps the greatest challenge to Urdu critics and intellectuals was thrown by Sara Shagufta who violated all the conventions and norms in her poetry. Piling image upon image in a multicoloured collage of words, she reflects meaning as if through a prism of deliberate obscurity and defiance. Her poems make no concessions to the sound values of words. She shuns metrical patterns, repetition, alliteration and smooth lyrical sounds, the devices commonly favoured by traditional Urdu poets, choosing to rely instead on clusters of images:

> I wake up in the fire
> echoing in the stone
> Drowning. What trees will grow from the earth
> Call my sorrows a child –
> in my hands are broken toys . . .
> and before my eyes a man
> countless bodies beg me for eyes . . .

Deeply pained by the cruel indifference of a chauvinistic poet husband who was surrounded by 'critics/friends' ready to deride her work, she challenges their double standards and unfair dominance. Whilst describing her own struggle as an artist in the USA, Judy Chicago records in her book, *Through the Flower*:

> There was no frame of reference in 1970 to understand a woman's struggle, to value it or to read and respond to the imagery that grew out of it . . . And even if the male world could acknowledge that struggle, could it even allow it to be considered 'important' art, as important as the art that grew out of men's lives? I could not be content with having my work seen as trivial, limited, or 'unimportant', if it dealt openly with my experiences as a woman.

I would argue that circumstances are not much better twenty years later. Chicago's experience typifies the obstacles still faced by women artists, writers and poets around the world. A recent publication from London, *Reviewing the Reviews* (Women in Publishing, 1987), reveals that of 53,000 titles reviewed annually by the *Times Literary Supplement* only 3,000 books (approximately) are by women. The self-appointed arbiters of taste and aesthetics are still men. They define the literary canons, build or wreck reputations, and, by largely ignoring women's writing, marginalise it. Sometimes the pain and suffering which that causes inflicts a fatal wound on a sensitive spirit. Sylvia Plath's experience in England in 1963 finds an echo in the suicidal death of Sara Shagufta in Karachi in 1984.

The Selection

This selection is meant to challenge some of those judgments. I believe that the most innovative, the most radical and the most interesting Urdu poetry of our times is being produced by women and not by male poets. Unless women begin to assume and assert their role as critics, there is a danger that this fact may remain obscure and unnoticed.

I have tried to bring the contemporary strain in Urdu poetry by women into this selection and to put across the strength of feminist feeling and conviction that rewarded my search. I decided early on that I would select poems which had a content of feminist struggle or political awareness. I knew that this might not always yield the best of a poet's work and that I would have to exclude Parveen Shakir and Ada Jaafri, two well-known and highly regarded women poets. Both women have chosen to confine themselves to poetry which is apolitical, sentimental and conformist. Parveen Shakir, who is younger and has also hosted a popular television series on poetry, has explored themes such as physical love in her poetry, but the acceptance of sexist values and the absence of a social context makes her writing distinctively un-feminist. Ada Jaafri's work is even more traditional than Shakir's.

My intention was to find the modern and the dynamic in women's Urdu poetry which would establish its relevance for the nineties. I reasoned that only those poets deserved to be included who had contributed something towards extending the frontiers of form and thought; those who had some original insights to offer, who represented that strand of the progressive tradition in Urdu poetry which had so powerfully contributed to the freedom movement in the early forties – a strand with a strong commitment to political action.

I was not seeking gems of individual value but a body of work that represented the mood of a generation of women in conflict with tradition and, to some extent, religion, as interpreted by men and expressed in Fundamentalist Islam. I found the courage and spirit within individual voices of protest impressive. Their rebellion, their self-conscious links with other artists, activists and writers involved in the movement, their need to challenge traditional forms, their interest in what women were writing in other languages across the world, were all aspects which I wanted to represent.

The term feminism is vague, elusive, and largely relative. As someone living in the West, who is constantly faced with the challenge of resolving the tensions between two quite diverse cultures, I am aware that it is a term that can straddle widely divergent attitudes. I have used the term here in its broadest sense: as an awareness of the disadvantages and constraints faced by women in a traditional society and a recognition of their need or the desire for freedom and change.

The most problematic for this definition might be the poems by Zehra Nigah. Is 'Compromise' a feminist or a feminine poem? There is a note of wistfulness, a knowledge of having been short-changed, a certain sad dissatisfaction which, with its understanding of the inevitable weaving together of the social and the personal in women's lives, raises it above the level of the purely personal. In its honest acceptance of defeat which was and is the lot of the traditional, conformist woman, it still manages to attain a certain dignity and poignancy. Similarly, 'My Crime: A Promise' expresses the sense of personal loss and suffering in a world where the individual is secondary. Fortunately, controversial choices like that are fewer in the collection in comparison with work that is overtly political and more uncompromisingly feminist. By and large the collection contains work that addressed itself directly or indirectly to the reactionary forces in Pakistan which were threatening to undermine women's denuded position even further.

There were at least three important reasons behind my decision to work on this collection. I wanted to highlight the work of women poets in Pakistan as a tribute to its innovative nature and intrinsic value. Secondly, I wanted to chart and project the role of these poets in the women's movement that was gathering momentum in the country, so as to dispel the assumption that women in the developing world are passive, voiceless and hopelessly conformist. Finally, for myself, I needed to restore my links with a part of my heritage that I had been in danger of losing. In doing so, I restore those links for a whole generation of women in the diaspora who need the translation to help them find their way through the original. This work gave me enormous strength at a time when I felt bleak about the status of women in Pakistan.

The Socio-political Context

The military regime led by General Zia-ul-Haque is not

solely responsible for the low status of women in that country, nor has his death brought it to an end. It is the result of centuries of subjugation of women in the subcontinent. His regime clearly decided to use the women's issue to control society in a much more repressive grip.

Nawal El Saadawi's definition of Fundamentalism is certainly apt in the case of Pakistan. It is a world phenomenon which:

> . . . operates under different religious slogans, but is a political movement using God to justify injustices and discriminate between people, nations, classes, races, sexes, colours and creeds . . .[1]

General Zia-ul-Haque, who had seized power in a military coup from Prime Minister Zulfikar Ali Bhutto in July 1977, had promised elections within ninety days. Less than two years later, Bhutto had been hanged, elections cancelled and political activity banned. During this time, a programme for Islamisation was carefully formulated and honed, then launched to gain support from right-wing elements for an otherwise unpopular regime which strongly promoted capital and free enterprise.

Broadly, the underlying objectives of the programme were to curtail democracy and establish a theocratic state which would be extremely difficult to dislodge. It was assumed by him, as it still is, by the IJI[2] (the coalition of parties led by Nawaz Sharif, now in power in Pakistan), that Islamisation had the potential for cementing a crumbling national identity. The Soviet invasion could not have been timed better to suit the political exigencies of the time, bringing in, as it did, substantial US aid and muffling international censure at a critical point. Thus the people of Pakistan were left isolated to suffer the excesses of this tyrannical process for eleven damaging years.

Ironically, the process itself had been begun in Bhutto's reign with a few laws, such as the Prohibition of Alcohol, the declaration of Friday as the holiday in the working week and the closure of Western-style discotheques. These laws were enacted by Bhutto as concessions to the right-wing opposition in a last bid to survive. These became insignificant, in hindsight, as personal freedoms were eroded by successive laws enforced in the name of Islam by General Zia.

The Islamic Ideology Council had been in place for some time with a brief to scrutinise existing laws which might be in contravention of Shariat (Muslim) laws. Women's groups were constantly being reassured by General Zia that the Family Laws Ordinance (1961) would not be repealed. This was a precious piece of legislation won by women in Ayub Khan's time which obtained limited protection from bigamy and some rights within marriage. In Zia's time it seemed vulnerable. In the event, its efficacy was reduced and women were left fighting legislation which was much more retrogressive and direct in its assault on their basic rights.

A nationwide media campaign entitled *Chadur aur Chardiwari* (the veil and four walls) was mounted to enforce the seclusion of women with *Nawaa-i-Waqt*, a leading Urdu daily, at its head. The government issued directives concerning the wearing of *chadurs* by television presenters and female government employees. This was followed by an 'anti-pornography' campaign which reduced the participation of women in television and entertainment. The Muslim parties knew that General Zia needed their support to continue in power and made full use of the collusion.

A serious attempt was made to deny educational opportunities to girls and young women. The minimum age for marriage, raised by the Family Laws Ordinance to eighteen years, was debated in an attempt to bring it, supposedly, into accordance with Islamic law. This defines the onset of puberty as a sign of maturity in girls and permits consummation of marriage at that age. Fortunately, pressure from the World Bank, which saw the implications of such a law for population increase, prevented this from being instituted.[3]

A campaign to relegate women to segregated universities also failed partly because of financial implications, partly through the realisation that women vastly outnumbered male students in Karachi University, partly owing to pressure from the women's groups who rightly saw this as a dangerous reduction of opportunities for women.

Whilst laws curtailing political activity and the promotion of the idea that only 'good Muslims' were eligible for testimony and public office affected all citizens, particularly the minorities in Pakistan, it gradually became apparent that women would be the subject of a major revival of oppressive laws.

The first real inkling of the seriousness of the problem came with the promulgation of the Hudood Ordinances on 10 February, 1979. These dealt with: theft, drunkenness, *Qazf* (bearing false witness) and, finally, *zina*, which included rape and adultery. The word *hadd* literally means boundary or limit and the term *hadd* implies a maximum penalty fixed by the Sharia for a particular offence.

Federal Shariat courts had been set up to speed up the process of Islamisation. These were special benches of each of the four High Courts and an appellate Shariat Bench at the Supreme Court.[4] They effectively implemented changes which the Islamic Ideology Council had previously been able only to recommend in an advisory role. Not only did the Shariat courts have the power to award or review the punishments designated by the Hudood Ordinances, they also had the power to review any law which anyone wishing to challenge 'un-Islamic' legislation could invoke through a petition.

The *hadd* for theft – amputation of the right hand for a first offence, and the left foot for a second one (if there were no extenuating circumstances) – had shocked most Pakistanis. The lower sessions court judges frequently made blundering judgments based on Hudood laws, provoking public outrage and women's fury. This left the higher Shariat benches to mop up the mess. Repeatedly, sentences were awarded by the lower courts only to be reversed by a higher court in recognition of public disgust. For the government it was easiest to use flogging (awarded for drunkenness, public order offences and other petty crimes) as a powerful political weapon to create an atmosphere of fear and to silence dissent.

The worst laws affecting the status of women were yet to come. Not everyone understood the full implications of the Hudood Ordinance, covering *zina*, when it was first announced. The offence of *zina* (adultery) by a married person carried the extreme penalty of death, and the *hadd* penalty of death by stoning. For an unmarried person the penalty was up to a hundred lashes. In practice, the law failed to distinguish clearly enough between fornication, adultery and rape. Rape, '*zina bil Jabr*', required the same testimony as adultery, that is, four adult male Muslims of good repute who testify to have seen the act of penetration. This made prosecution of rape impossible under this law. (However, ordinary civil law continued to be applied to rape cases and charges could be brought against offenders, and indeed were, during the Zia years.) But an attempt was made in some of the lower courts to use this piece of legislation against women, to subvert the due process of law and punish the victim. Specially at risk were unmarried women who became pregnant and who could, therefore, be held guilty of unlawful intercourse. This led to some absurd sentences and was subject to misuse by the police and civil authorities against working-class women who were less able to protect their own interests.

It was not until the autumn of 1982 when a couple, Fehmida and Allah Bux, were awarded the *hadd* punishment of death by stoning that women were finally jolted into action. Shirkat Gah, a women's pressure group based in Karachi, began the process by calling a meeting of all women's groups and inviting them to act to protect women's rights. Women's Action Forum was launched with an emphasis on action; two months later the Lahore chapter was set up and Islamabad, Rawalpindi and Peshawar soon followed suit. Women in the Forum were drawn from a range of organisations. In its infancy, the movement suffered from bitter wrangling and power struggles but nevertheless gathered momentum. WAF's great achievement was to obtain the endorsement of APWA (All Pakistan Women's Association), the oldest, broad-based, centrist women's organisation in Pakistan. Many APWA members had fought in the freedom movement alongside men and had expected equal rights in the new country. The realisation that even existing freedoms were now to be taken away instead of being extended, shocked them. Begum Raana Liaquat Ali, the Chair of APWA, gave the resistance her blessing, which was important and valuable. WAF had decided to appeal on behalf of Fehmida and Allah Bux but Khalid Ishaq, a leading expert in Islamic Jurisprudence, took on the case and succeeded in obtaining a dismissal.

Two years later, women's groups in Lahore, active and vigilant, were more readily mobilised when the case of Safia Bibi, a near-blind working-class woman, drew public attention. She had been raped by a landlord and his son in whose home she was employed as a domestic servant. Her father had registered a rape case against them after the birth of her illegitimate baby, who died. The sessions judge had taken it upon himself to award her punishment under the Zina Ordinance: fifteen lashes, three years of imprisonment and a fine of Rs.1000 (in his view, a mild sentence) whilst finding her rapists not guilty owing to lack of evidence, under the same law. Women, shocked and horrified, managed to co-ordinate, a sophisticated media campaign, as well as a defence which led the government into considerable embarrassment at an international level, and a prompt dismissal of the case by the Federal Shariat High Court followed.

Women now recognised clearly that:

> As the law stands it protects rapists, prevents women from testifying and confuses the issue of rape with adultery. [5]

Their next step was to challenge the legislation in a court of law, which they did. A team of eminent lawyers including Rashida Patel [6] and Khalid Ishaq represented them, but, by the time the case was heard (1985) by the Federal Shariat Court, the Eighth Amendment had rendered it null and void.

Seven years later, the martial law had changed its strategy, attained a semi-legal status through elections contested on a non-party basis and was making far-reaching changes in the laws through the so-called 'elected representatives'. The free world media image of General Zia was no longer that of a villain, but that of a champion of the Afghan Mujahideen struggling for liberation from their Soviet invaders.

Stoning had never been instituted or practised in Pakistan before 1979, nor has it been allowed to happen since. There are no verifiable records of its practice amongst Muslims since early times, even in Saudi Arabia. The idea is repugnant to many Pakistanis, both men and women, and sentences have in the past been revoked, as a response to campaigns. But the laws remain on the statute books and can be used to harass ordinary people.

Even now casework is undertaken by women's groups who need to support those members of the public, mostly women who are still vulnerable and may find themselves trapped in the iniquitous Hudood laws through personal enmities or official malice. Zehra Nigah's poem 'Hudood Ordinance' refers to such an innocent victim.

Najma Sadeque's hard work drew public attention to several instances of extreme cruelty and injustice against women during the Zia years. A founder member of Karachi WAF and a successful journalist, she makes perceptive comments about the nature of oppression against women in an article entitled 'The Importance of Stoning a Woman', published in a leading Pakistani daily newspaper, *Dawn* (Karachi), in 1987:

> It is power that is imposed against public will that has to turn intimidatory and ugly to enforce itself. The act of stoning a woman to death would be a manifestation of that power sanctioned to give fangs to functionary power at the social level ... the stoning of a woman is a means of declaring (as do all other arbitrary sentences, ordinances and directives) as to who calls the shots, driving the message home with anticipated paralysing effect.

As the country veered further towards Saudi influence, the Ahmediya Muslims were excommunicated and hounded, being declared non-Muslims. Clearly then, Najma Sadeque's assessment is valid. Through these laws force against women was being used to control the rest of society more effectively. Two poems in this collection deal directly with stoning: Fahmida Riaz's 'Stoning' (written before the promulgation of the law) and Neelma Sarwar's 'I Wish That Day of Judgment Would Come'. Neelma Sarwar deals with public flogging in 'To the First Man to Be Awarded Lashes'.

Women were constantly waging battles against all these retrogressive changes but the issue which galvanised them into action was the Law of Evidence. This was designed to curtail the civic rights and stature of women as individuals by declaring the testimony of one woman as insufficient evidence unless supported by another woman. In effect it valued the testimony of one woman as worth half that of a man. The absurdity of this law and fears that it might be a step towards disenfranchising them brought women out on a march in Lahore on 12 February 1982, led by professional women. It was, at best, a group of 200 or so but police reacted with fierce and disproportionate violence; tear gas, baton charges and arrests followed. Saeeda Gazdar's 'Twelfth of February, 1983' is based on this episode of the struggle.

The slant of the laws against women began to have a subtle but clearly visible effect on society. There were obvious changes, for example, in the way women were dressing and behaving. Young couples were stopped and harassed if the police thought that they might be courting. Bigamy, illegal and socially taboo since the Family Laws Ordinance (except by permission of the first wife), came back in through the back door as the local Union Councils who implemented the law disappeared and were not replaced. Kishwar Naheed makes reference to permission papers in her poem 'Section 144' which bemoans the times.

As time went on, the Islamisation campaign had the effect of escalating violence against women. The Women's Action Forum recorded and drew attention to the rising statistics of crimes, brutality and mistreatment of women. Their activism prevented some of these atavistic laws from being instituted. For example, the Law of Evidence, fought by women so heroically in its draft form, had to change in its final form. It was decided that it would only be applied to documented agreements concerning financial dealings and commercial contracts and not be used as a blanket law covering all situations involving women's testimony.

Nevertheless, the damage had been done. Cultural events became men-only affairs with music, singing and dancing virtually disappearing from the stages. Television became a powerful weapon of religious propaganda, blaring out the virtues of prayer and asceticism whilst the rich got richer and the poor groaned under a spiralling rate of inflation. Posters drove home messages of fear of God and death in a time-bound material world. Artists sold their paint brushes for calligraphy pens. Only a handful of women artists continued to paint with an awareness of the political context and a fiercely heightened sense of the oppression of women. Amongst them were Salima Hashmi and Naazish Ataullah, both of whom have, appropriately, worked on cover designs for Kishwar Naheed's books.

During her brief tenure as Prime Minister, Benazir Bhutto did not change or challenge any of the legislation affecting women; nor did she seem able to contest the indirect domination or social control by men which was expressed in the changed fashions and the donning of veils. She fought the election sporting a veil herself, something she had never done before, and has not been able to shed it since. She is careful never to be seen in Western garments and, unlike her younger self, dresses in the prescribed Islamic manner. Her successor, Nawaz Sharif, was brought to power through a coalition which includes the religious parties, and so would be expected to follow, at least ostensibly, the trend towards Islamisation.

The recent enactment of the Shariat Bill demonstrates a shrewd compromise which has left both fundamentalist extremists and liberals unhappy, but which has resolved a long-standing problem. It has transformed the original Bill – which would have made Parliament redundant and considerably weakened the executive since it was designed to replace the constitution of Pakistan with Shariat laws – into a new, benign version which leaves legislative power firmly in the hands of the National Assembly and makes all revisions in the direction of Islamisation subject to the will of the Assembly. The Islamic parties did not do well at the polls and the likelihood of retrogressive changes now seems smaller, though it cannot be overruled. Women's groups have maintained a judicious silence. A climate has nevertheless been created which makes progressive changes in the laws affecting women less likely.

Poetry in Urdu is not the exclusive property of the cultural élite. Poetry readings, or *mushai'ras*, are an established and popular convention for Urdu speakers and attract many people who may not otherwise view themselves as 'literary' or who may not be in the habit of buying books. As some of this poetry is also set to music and sung, its use for political influence cannot be underestimated. Poets can, therefore, become targets for political persecution, as indeed Riaz and Naheed were. Iqbal had made direct political use of his poetry during the struggle for freedom by reciting at political rallies. Pakistani women are now using this convention too, consciously and effectively.

Some of the poets in the collection have strong links with the women's movement; they have read, recited and published work for women's groups to mark occasions such as International Women's Day and at rallies. There were also campaign poems, jingles and anthems, poetry of a more accessible style, published in newsletters or pamphlets which have not been included here. In some ways Saeeda Gazdar's poem, 'Twelfth of February, 1983' which has its value as social history, belongs to this category.

This collection thus represents a new wave of self-aware and highly politicised women poets who understand the dimensions of the battle on their hands and whose work is concerned with women's issues and informed with careful, sensitive thought. These women may be in a small minority but it is one which is vocal. Many of them have consciously undertaken formal studies of women's deprivation and political issues in Pakistan. They sustain, respect and validate each other's work, realising that there is a large block of support, silent and invisible though it may be. This volume serves as a tribute to their work and to the women's movement in Pakistan.

A Word About the Translation

At a literary event honouring him in London, the Soviet poet Rasul Gamzatov, who writes in a 'minor' language from the Ukraine and speaks no English himself, described receiving poetry in translation as an experience comparable to looking at the wrong side of a carpet. It is a harsh judgment but it contains an element of truth. There is no doubt a serious loss of some of the qualities essential to poetry in the best of translations for which there is no easy substitute. Yet, in a much smaller and still much-divided world, translations are an invaluable tool for deepening understanding, appreciation and tolerance for cultures that may be at variance with each other.

The greater the differences in the cultural mores of two societies the harder it is for a translator to do justice to the original. Again, the finer the poem, the richer it is in terms of suggestions, references, emotional innuendos and subtleties and the harder it becomes to translate it well.

My technique has been to rely heavily on the imagery and to stay as loyal to that as possible. Wherever the images are free of special cultural referents the reader would have as close an experience of the poem as is possible without knowing the language; however, often there is a complex overlay of a culturally defined context and only a transfer of images is not enough. There are other clues to the meaning which I have used in such poems. I have not restricted myself to abiding by the word order in the original since Urdu is a 'free word order' language and that often translates into extremely awkward constructions in English. I have attempted a sense of rhyme and rhythm but not as a religious rite for every poem, only as a means of conveying its essential quality in the original. A poem such as Zehra Nigah's 'The Moonflower Tree' would suffer too much if reduced to free verse. I have tried to evolve some kind of a rhyming pattern for *ghazals* as I felt this is quite essential to their nature. It works better in some instances than it does in others but even if it conveys partially the wonderful satisfaction of a genre that is highly symmetrical, formal and richly melodious, it serves the purpose.

Unlike English, metrical patterns in Urdu depend on line lengths and lengths of syllables rather than on stresses. There is no preordained word order and punctuation is seldom used. I have introduced some punctuation where it is necessary.

I decided that I preferred footnotes along with the original Urdu words in some instances to mismatched, unsatisfactory English equivalents and feel that the explanation in each instance will justify my judgment to the reader. Some of the footnotes clarify a political or historical reference.

THE POETS

Kishwar Naheed

If there is a Pakistani feminist who poses a serious threat to men through her work, her lifestyle, her manner and through ceaseless verbal challenge, it is Kishwar Naheed. She does this with a professional dedication which either endears or enrages, there are no half-measures. At forty-seven, widowed, mother of two grown sons, completely independent financially, she is above many strictures that other women in Pakistan would have to observe, those which remain she flouts with a relish.

She held a powerful position above her peers as the editor of a prestigious monthly, *Maah-i-Nau*, for several years, which meant that many of her male colleagues have had to put up with her cultivated stroppiness however much they may have resented it. This government publication has acquired its reputation for editorial independence and literary quality over several years and through the hard work of several progressive editors. Whilst Kishwar was editor she was charged with various offences on thirty different occasions. One of these was a charge of obscenity brought against her after she published an abridged version of Simone de Beauvoir's *The Second Sex*. She won the court battle and managed to have her grade as an officer restored which had been stripped as a punishment.

Kishwar has been no stranger to controversy. At twenty she married Yusuf Kamraan, a classmate and fellow poet (who was later to become a television celebrity), against the wishes of her family, dropped out of her final year of Economics and went to work to support him through *his* final year. Their marriage remained unconventional but the relationship appears to be somewhat ambivalent, a far cry from the fairy-tale ending the youthful poets in love might have expected it to be. A strong streak of cynicism runs through the personal poetry of both poets in later years.

Kishwar is perhaps the most prolific poet of her generation. As her writing became more political, developing rapidly partly because of her determination to expand her work and partly in response to the political climate in Pakistan which became increasingly repressive towards women after Bhutto's deposition, Kishwar's reputation grew. Her poetry thrived on the persecution she was subjected to as a civil servant. Her search for growth led her to a detailed study of progressive contemporary poets from several countries, many of whom she translated into Urdu in a volume which is often accused of having been put together too hastily.

Kishwar's free verse and style have been criticised for lack of polish, for 'shoddiness', but what is missing in terms of poetic craft is compensated for adequately by her enormous range, boundless energy and uninhibited, honest exploration of themes. Her poems range from traditional love poems written in the early years to those dealing with hysterectomy, male chauvinism, censorship, American intervention in Pakistan and a host of feminist issues.

To date, her work includes several volumes of poetry: *Lips that Speak*, *Unnamed Journey*, *Poems*, *Alleyways: the Sun: Doorways*, *Amidst Reproaches*, *Complete Poems* and *The Colour Pink within a Black Border*. Her prose work *Woman 'twixt Dreams and Dust* deals with Pakistani women's issues in depth: images of women in the media and textbooks, crimes against women, rape, abortion, women in agriculture, women and politics, the role of religion and the controversial family laws of Pakistan. She has also published *Come Back Africa*, the story of Laila Khalid, and *Women in the Mirror of Psychology*. Two collections of Kishwar Naheed's poems have been translated into English.

Fahmida Riaz

Fahmida Riaz, who graduated from Sindh University and married in 1965, has published several volumes of poetry.

During the Martial Law regime she was editor and publisher of the magazine, *Awaaz*. In all, fourteen court cases of sedition were filed against the magazine, one of which (under section 114 A) carried a death penalty. She escaped to India whilst on bail, with her husband and two children, where she lived for seven years. She worked as Poet-in-Residence at Jamia Millia, an Indian university, during this period.

She has translated Erich Fromme's *Fear of Freedom* and Sheikh Ayaz's poetry, from Sindhi into Urdu. Since the restoration of democracy she has returned to live in Pakistan and served as Director General of Pakistan's National Book Council in Islamabad when Benazir Bhutto's Pakistan People's Party was in power.

Her book, *The Body Lacerated*, caused tremendous controversy because of its uninhibited and vigorous exploration of female sexuality. A woman in traditional Urdu poetry is a concept, not a person . . . an ideal with rosy cheeks, shining black eyes concealed shyly under long, dark eyelashes and a shapely swaying body. Fahmida rejects that passive virginal model in favour of a living, throbbing, vocal and passionate reality.

Her greatest contribution to literature is her recognition of the role of language in society. She has some interesting insights to offer, particularly with regard to the history of the Urdu language. She is committed to modifying the choice of diction which is current and accepted in established circles of Urdu poetry. She brings to her poetry her conviction that literary Urdu, too closely associated with the Persianised Imperial Court, had lost its nutritive sources as a living language of the people, by losing touch with its roots. Since the sustenance, relevance and contemporaneity of a language must derive from its living usage, not from books and papers, her argument is valid. Languages which cut off links with their grass-roots communities have been known to become emaciated, and do, invariably, die. She herself struggles in her language to restore its links with the usage of peasants and workers.

Riaz has moved away from the *ghazal* form but her poems resonate with music and her success as a lyricist is widely acknowledged. She has published *My Crime Is Proven*, *Will You Not See the Full Moon?*, *Sun*, *Stones that Speak* and *I Am a Statue of Clay*.

Sara Shagufta

The late Sara Shagufta, who committed suicide tragically young after tremendous personal suffering, rejected the role models and literary images of women more completely than any other poet represented in this collection. She defies the poetic traditions of Urdu, inverting, bending, subverting, challenging all the rules. Her work is rich in terms of imagery, originality and sheer poetic energy. Perhaps the tragic depths of her experience are best represented in her own words. 'The Last Word' is the title of a biographical letter appended to her only collection of poems, *Eyes*. It describes very baldly some traumatic moments in her life. I have translated a short excerpt:

> When the pains got worse the landlady heard me screaming and left me at the hospital. 'I held five crackling notes and the pain in my hands.'
> After some time a boy was born. It was bitterly cold and there was not even a towel to wrap the child.
> The doctor placed the baby beside me on the stretcher.
> For five minutes the baby opened its eyes and then left to earn itself a coffin.
> Since that day my body feels full of eyes.

Sister showed me into the ward. I told her I want to go home because at home no one knows where I am. She glared at me and said it may be dangerous for me to rush around, that I should stay in bed. But I could not rest after that.

I had a dead baby and five rupees.

'It is difficult for me to stay in hospital now. I haven't got the money for the fee. I'll fetch it. I won't run away. You can keep my dead baby as a surety.'

I had a temperature of 105 degrees. I got on to the bus and went home. My breasts were overflowing. I filled a glass with milk and kept it on the table. The poet and the other scribes returned. I said to the poet, 'I gave birth to a boy but he has died.'

He heard it casually and mentioned it to his critics.

There was silence in the room for two minutes.

The conversation resumed in the third minute.

What do you think of Freud?

What does Rimbaud say?

What has Saadi said?

Warris Shah was the greatest.

I used to hear these things every day but the words sounded clearer today.

As if all these great people had stopped in my blood for a little while. And as if Rimbaud and Freud were snatching my baby from my womb. That day Knowledge entered my home for the first time and was screaming with laughter in my blood. Look at the birth of my child!

Zehra Nigah

Zehra Nigah is a much-loved and highly respected poet in Pakistan, but although she has written for several years she has published only one volume of poetry: *The First Star of Twilight*. This single volume spans three distinct periods in her writing and demonstrates her skills as an accomplished lyricist and a fine poet capable of both intensity and subtlety. The slimness of this volume speaks eloquently of the precedence she gave to domesticity over poetry: a heroic sacrifice but one that was evidently not without pain. Zehra Nigah's work is quite traditional, both in form and content. Her reputation owes much to her elegant phrasing and a highly cultivated style of presentation which enthrals audiences at poetry readings. The poems included here illustrate the pathos of her resignation. They acknowledge the power of the forces to which women must submit in sharp contrast with the energy and anger apparent in the work of the more political poets like Kishwar Naheed and Fahmida Riaz. They are also interesting in as much as they stay well within the bounds of 'protest' expected and permitted in women's writing from the subcontinent.

Zehra Nigah lives in London, where she occasionally appears at literary events.

Ishrat Aafreen

Ishrat Aafreen is the youngest and one of the lesser-known poets in the collection. She has worked as assistant editor for a monthly magazine, *Awaaz*. Her only volume of poems, *A Grove of Yellow Flowers*, is remarkable for a first offering. It has been awarded condescending approval in an introduction by Ali Sardar Jaafri.

She is the most literary of the poets in this collection, in terms of style; almost archaic in her observation of traditional norms, her use of language, and the most subtle in perception and argument. Perhaps on her shoulders the mantle of Faiz's tradition sits most comfortably. She herself identifies strongly with the poet Iqbal. A poem paying tribute to him describes him as a tree growing inside her. Her concept of Ego perhaps derives from Iqbal's concept of the Self. As opposed to its somewhat negative meaning in English, Aafreen uses the Urdu equivalent of the word ego to represent the individual self engaged in defiant and courageous battle with society.

It is curiously satisfying to see this highly polished traditional style in the service of a philosophy that is individual and rebellious. Her *ghazals* in the collection perhaps best illustrate this point. Aafreen's recognition of the cruelty to which women are subject is unambiguous and strong and her use of traditional metaphors heightens this sense of oppression by clinching the mechanics of that oppression with unfaltering clarity. She identifies how that which is upheld as heroic, pure and virtuous womanhood actually destroys and consumes women.

Aafreen married soon after the publication of her first volume of poetry and left Pakistan briefly to live in India. She has not published since, as if to confirm the 'poison of all the traditions' she writes about.

Saeeda Gazdar

Saeeda Gazdar worked as editor of a literary magazine, *Pakistani Adab*, for three years. She has also worked as a research associate at the Goethe Institute. She has published a novel entitled *The Boatman's Wife* and a collection of short stories, *The Fire Never Bloomed into a Garden*. Several of her articles, stories and poems have been published in newspapers and she has written scripts for documentary films, a couple of which were shown internationally. She is publishing another novel and a further collection of short stories. She has written two volumes of poems, *Chains of*

Days and Nights and *Gallows and Millstones*.

She has fought for women's rights and freedom in Pakistan not only through her writing but also through direct political action.

Neelma Sarwar

Neelma Sarwar is a graduate in Journalism who is now serving as a Deputy Superintendent for the police force in Lahore. She has published one volume of poetry, *Tongues of Stone*.

Most of the poems in her collection are personal. It is, however, significant that a poet who is not particularly feminist in her attitudes should have chosen to write at least a few poems which deal with the phase of repression that the country was undergoing. It also demonstrates that the women's movement has begun to raise the level of both political awareness and comment in certain sections of society.

In her work as a police officer she would, of course, have been in direct contact with the recipients of the awful punishments the government was handing out. All four poems represented in this collection deal with the theme of guilt and punishment.

ACKNOWLEDGMENTS

I am grateful to all the poets who made this work possible and have kindly allowed the use of their poetry for publication. I would like to thank all my dear friends and colleagues who have helped and supported me in many different ways. I am particularly grateful to Professor Ralph Russell, Iftikhar Arif, Ronald Warwick, Ranjana Ash and John Welch for their comments on the manuscript and generous support; to Roomana Mahmud for instigating the work and last, but not least, to my family for their patient and unwavering support.

The Women's Press and I gratefully acknowledge the support of the Arts Council for a grant to pay for the translation of the poems. Special thanks are due to Antonia Byatt and Alastair Niven.

NOTES

1. Nawal El Saadawi, *Fundamentalism on the Rise, Spare Rib* 202, June 1989.

2. IJI (Islami Jamhoori Itehad) is a working coalition of some Muslim League sections with Muslim parties, headed by Nawaz Sharif, a key opposition figure and chief minister of the Punjab, who was also governor of the Punjab in Gen Zia-ul-Haque's last years.

3. For a detailed discussion of this see: Lucy Carroll, *Nizam-I-Islam*, with special reference to the Position of Women in *The Journal of Commonwealth and Comparative Politics*, vol xx, no 1.

4. *Introduction of Hudood Laws in Pakistan*, Pakistan Publications, Islamabad 1979.

5. Farida Shaheed and Khawar Mumtaz, *Women of Pakistan*. Zed Books, London 1987, p 101.

6. Rashida Patel: author of two important books, *Islamisation of Laws in Pakistan* Saad, Karachi 1986 and *Women and Law in Pakistan*, Faiza, Karachi, 1979.

7. *Dawn*, Karachi.

ہم گنہگار عورتیں

یہ ہم گنہگار عورتیں ہیں
جو اہلِ جبہ کی تمکنت سے
نہ رعب کھائیں
نہ جان بیچیں
نہ سر جھکائیں
نہ ہاتھ جوڑیں

یہ ہم گنہگار عورتیں ہیں
کہ جن کے جسموں کی فصل بیچیں جو لوگ
وہ سرفراز ٹھہریں
نیابتِ امتیاز ٹھہریں
وہ داورِ اہلِ ساز ٹھہریں

یہ ہم گنہگار عورتیں ہیں
کہ سچ کا پرچم اٹھا کے نکلیں
تو جھوٹ سے شاہراہیں اٹی ملے ہیں
ہر ایک دہلیز پہ سزاؤں کی داستانیں دھری ملے ہیں
جو بول سکتی تھیں وہ زبانیں کٹی ملے ہیں

یہ ہم گنہگار عورتیں ہیں
کہ اب تعاقب میں رات بھی آئے
تو یہ آنکھیں نہیں بجھیں گی۔
کہ اب جو دیوار گر چکی ہے
اسے اٹھانے کی ضد نہ کرنا!

۳۰

We Sinful Women

It is we sinful women
who are not awed by the grandeur of those who wear
gowns

who don't sell our lives
who don't bow our heads
who don't fold our hands together.

It is we sinful women
while those who sell the harvests of our bodies
become exalted
become distinguished
become the just princes of the material world.

It is we sinful women
who come out raising the banner of truth
up against barricades of lies on the highways
who find stories of persecution piled on each threshold
who find the tongues which could speak have been
severed.

It is we sinful women.
Now, even if the night gives chase
these eyes shall not be put out.
For the wall which has been razed
don't insist now on raising it again.

یہ ہم گنہگار عورتیں ہیں
جو اہلِ جبّہ کی تمکنت سے نہ رعب کھائیں
نہ جان بیچیں
نہ سر جھکائیں ، نہ ہاتھ جوڑیں !

کشور ناہید

It is we sinful women
who are not awed by the grandeur of those who wear
gowns
who don't sell our bodies
who don't bow our heads
who don't fold our hands together.

KISHWAR NAHEED

دفعہ ۱۴۴

ہم اندیشے پن کے متلاشی ہیں
جہاں تمیز کی حدیں غائب ہو جاتی ہیں
اور ہم صرف لمس بن کر رہ جاتے ہیں،
لمس ۔ جو معذرت اور التجا کا آئینہ ہے
یہاں غربت اور امیری رہے گی
اس لئے کہ ہم ذہنوں کو چھو کر انہیں بے قیمت کر دیتے ہیں ۔
درخت پتے پہنتے ہیں
مگر خزاں، وصال کی شہوتوں میں انہیں دو زر کر دیتی ہے
ہم بہرے پن کے متلاشی ہیں
کہ جہاں لفظ و معنی، صرف جلتے لبوں کی جنبش میں
قید ہوتے ہیں
جنبش ۔۔۔۔۔ کٹھ پتلیوں کے تار ذرا بھی غلط ہل جائیں
تو سارا کھیل چوپٹ ہو جاتا ہے
یہ کھیل تو رہے گا
اندر کے خوف کو عصمت بننے دو
ہم گونگے پن کے متلاشی ہیں
کہ تالی بجانے والے آواز استعمال نہیں کرتے ہیں
آواز آزاد ہو تو نعرہ منصور
اور گھٹ جائے تو حسن ناصر بن جاتی ہے
مگر گونگے چیخ تو سکتے ہیں
یہ کیوں ہے ۔ یہ کیوں ممکن ہے !!

کشور ناہید

۳۴

Section 144*

We seek blindness
where the limits of discernment disappear
and we become merely a touch
Touch which is a mirror of apology and entreaty.
Here poverty and wealth shall remain
because we touch minds and render them valueless.
Trees wear leaves
but, lusting for union, Autumn buries them
                                        underground.
We seek deafness
where words and meanings are held captive
merely by the motion of moving lips.
Movement – if puppet strings move a trifle incorrectly
the entire show collapses.
This show will go on.
Don't let your inner fears turn to an uncontrollable
                                                  tremor.
We wish to be mute
for those who clap do not use their voices
A voice that is independent is the cry of Mansur**
When it is suffocated it becomes Naasir***
But at least the mute can scream
Why is that so? How is that possible?

                                                  KISHWAR NAHEED

*A section of the law used to prohibit public assemblies.
**Mansur was executed for insisting: 'I am God' in a mystical trance.
***A civil servant punished for speaking out against the government.

موم محل

میرے بیاہ سے پہلے میری ماں
خواب میں ڈر جایا کرتی تھی
اس کی خوفناک چیخوں سے میری آنکھ کھل جاتی تھی
میں اسے جگاتی ، ماجرا پوچھتی
اور وہ خالی آنکھوں گھورتی رہتی
اسے خواب یاد نہیں رہتے تھے
ایک رات خواب میں ڈر کر
اس نے چیخ نہیں ماری
خوف زدہ ہو کر مجھے اپنے ساتھ چمٹا لیا تھا
میں نے ماجرا پوچھا
تو اس نے آنکھیں کھول کر شکرانہ ادا کرتے ہوئے کہا
"میں نے خواب میں دیکھا تھا
تم ڈوب رہی ہو اور میں نے تمہیں بچانے کو دریا میں چھلانگ لگائی ہے"
اور اس رات بجلی گرنے سے
ہماری بھینس اور میرا منگیتر جل گئے تھے ۔
ایک رات ماں سو رہی تھی اور میں جاگ رہی تھی ،
ماں بار بار مٹھی بند کرتی اور کھولتی
اور یوں لگتا کہ جیسے کچھ پکڑنے کی کوشش میں تھک کر

۳۶

A Palace of Wax

Before I ever married
my mother
used to have
nightmares.
Her fearful screams shook me
I would wake her, ask her
'What happened?'
Blank-eyed she would stare at me.
She couldn't remember her dreams.

One day a nightmare woke her
but she did not scream
She held me tight in silent fear
I asked her,
'What happened?'
She opened her eyes and thanked the heavens
'I dreamt that you were drowning,'
she said,
'And I jumped into the river to save you.'

That night the lightning
killed our buffalo and my fiancé.

Then one night my mother slept
And I stayed up
Watching her open and shut her fist
She was trying to hold on to something

مگر پھر ہمت باندھنے کو مٹھی بند کرتی ہے
میں نے ماں کو جگایا
مگر ماں نے مجھے خواب بتانے سے انکار کر دیا ۔
اس دن سے میری نیند اڑ گئی
میں دوسرے صحن میں آگئی
اب میں اور میری ماں دونوں خواب میں چھینیں مارتے ہیں
اور جب کوئی پوچھے
تو کہہ دیتے ہیں
ہمیں خواب یاد نہیں رہتے ۔

کشور ناہید

Failing, and willing herself to hold on again.

I woke her
But she refused to tell me her dream.

Since that day
I have not slept soundly.
I moved to the other courtyard.

Now I and my mother both scream
through our nightmares

And if someone asks us
We just tell them
We can't remember our dreams.

                                        KISHWAR NAHEED

گھاس تو مجھ جیسی ہے

گھاس تو مجھ جیسی ہے
پاؤں تلے بچھ کر ہی، زندگی کی مراد پاتی ہے
مگر یہ بھئی! کر کس بات کی گواہی بنتی ہے
شرمساری کی آنچ کی
کہ جذبے کی حدت کی
گھاس بھی مجھ جیسی ہے
ذرا سر اٹھانے کے قابل ہو
تو کاٹنے والی مشین
اسے مخمل بنانے کا سودا لئے
ہموار کرتی رہتی ہے
عورت کو بھی ہموار کرنے کے لئے
تم کیسے کیسے جتن کرتے ہو۔
نہ زمین کی نمو کی خواہش مرتی ہے
نہ عورت کی
میری مانو، تو وہی پگڈنڈی بنانے کا خیال درست تھا
جو عضلوں کی شکستوں کی آنچ نہ سہہ سکیں
وہ پیوندِ زمین ہو کر
یونہی زور آوروں کے لئے راستہ بنا دیتے ہیں
مگر وہ پر کاہ ہیں
گھاس نہیں
گھاس تو مجھ جیسی ہے!

کشور ناہید

The Grass Is Really Like Me

The grass is also like me
it has to unfurl underfoot to fulfil itself
but what does its wetness manifest:
a scorching sense of shame
or the heat of emotion?

The grass is also like me
As soon as it can raise its head
the lawnmower,
obsessed with flattening it into velvet,
mows it down again.
How you strive and endeavour
to level woman down too!
But neither the earth's nor woman's
desire to manifest life dies.
Take my advice: the idea of making a footpath was a
                                           good one.
Those who cannot bear the scorching defeat of their
                                               courage
are grafted on to the earth.
That's how they make way for the mighty
but they are merely straw   not grass
– the grass is really like me.

                                          KISHWAR NAHEED

میں کون ہوں

موزے بیچتی جوتے بیچتی عورت میرا نام نہیں
میں تو وہی ہوں جس کو تم دیواریں چن کر
مثلِ صبا بے خوف ہونے
یہ نہیں جانا
پتھر سے آواز کبھی بھی دب نہیں سکتی
میں تو وہی ہوں رسم و رواج کے بوجھ تلے
جسے تم نے چھپایا
یہ نہیں جانا
روشنی گھور اندھیروں سے کبھی ڈر نہیں سکتی
میں تو وہی ہوں گود ہے جس کی پھول چنے
انگارے اور کانٹے ڈالے
یہ نہیں جانا
زنجیروں سے پھولوں کی خوشبو چھپ نہیں سکتی
میں تو وہی ہوں میری حیا کے نام پہ تم نے
مجھ کو خریدا مجھ کو بیچا
یہ نہیں جانا
کچے گھڑے پہ تیرے سوہنی مر نہیں سکتی

Who Am I?

I am not that woman selling socks and shoes

I am the one you needed to bury alive
to feel fearless as the wind again
For you never knew
that stones can never suppress a voice.

I am the one you hid beneath
the weight of traditions
For you never knew
that light can never fear pitch darkness.

I am the one from whose lap you picked flowers
and then poured flames and thorns instead
For you never knew
that chains cannot hide the fragrance of flowers.

In the name of modesty
you bought and sold me
For you never knew
that Sohni* cannot die braving the river on a fragile
                                                              pot of clay.

---

*A famous Punjabi legend. Sohni would cross the River Chenab on a baked clay pot every night to meet her lover. This pot was substituted by her sister-in-law for an unbaked one, causing her to drown.

میں تو وہی ہوں جسے کو تم نے ڈو بی بٹھا کے
اپنے سرسے بوجھ اتارا
یہ نہیں جانا
ذہن غلام اگر ہے قوم ابھر نہیں سکتی
پہلے تم نے میری شرم و حیا پہ خوب تجارت کی تھی
میری ممتا ، میری وفا کے نام پر خوب تجارت کی تھی
اب گو دو ہیں اور ذہنوں میں پھولوں کے کھلنے کا موسم ہے
پوسٹروں پر پریم برہمنہ
موزے بیچتی جوتے بیچتی عورت میرا نام نہیں

کشور ناہید

I am the one you gave away in marriage
So you could be rid of me
For you never knew
that a nation cannot emerge if the mind is enslaved.

For a long time you have profited by my shyness and
modesty
Traded so well on my motherhood and fidelity,
Now the season for flowers to bloom in our laps and
minds is here.

Semi-naked on the posters –
I am not that woman – selling socks and shoes.

KISHWAR NAHEED

"نائٹ میر"

کبری : ذبح ہونے کا انتظار کرتی ہے
اور میں صبح ہونے کا ۔
کیوں کہ روز دفتر کی میز پر ذبح ہوتی ہوں
جھوٹ بولنے کے لئے
یہی میری قیمت ہے ۔
تازہ قبروں کی طرح پاؤڈر سے لپے ہوئے چہرے
مجھے ملنے آتے ہیں
ذہنوں کے قبرستان میں ایسی سجاوٹیں ہی
زیب دیتی ہیں
میں اور میرا وطن ایک ساتھ پیدا ہوئے تھے
مگر دونوں کی بغارت بچپن ہی میں ماری گئی ۔
میں نے روٹی دیکھی نہیں
اپنے تصور میں اس کی شکل بناتی اور کھاتی ہوں
میرے بہت سے ہم عمر ، روٹی صرف خواب میں دیکھتے ہیں ۔
میرے ملک میں عورتیں پہلی کا چاند دیکھ کر دعائیں مانگتی ہیں
اور باقی ساری دعائیں اگلی پہلی کے لئے اٹھا رکھتی ہیں ۔
دوسری شادی کے اجازت نامے پہ انگوٹھا لگانے کے بعد
بھی
وہ پہلی کا چاند دیکھ کر دعائیں مانگتی رہتی ہیں ۔
شاید ہم جیسے جھوٹ بولنے والوں کی عاقبت سنوارنے کے لئے ۔

Nightmare

The goat awaits slaughter
and I wait for the morning
for every morning I am slaughtered at my office desk
for telling lies.
This is my price.

Like fresh graves,
faces smoothly caked with powder
come to meet me
In the graveyard of minds only such adornments seem
                                                appropriate.

I and my country were born together
but we both lost our vision in our childhood.
I have not seen bread.
In my imagination I picture it and eat it.
A number of my generation dreams only of bread.

In my country women look at the crescent moon and
                                                        pray
And shelve all the rest of their prayers for the first day
                                              of the next moon.
Even after they have stamped permits for a second
                                    marriage with their own thumbs
they pray when they see the first moon of the month.
Perhaps, to attain a better afterlife for liars like
                                                         us.

ہم اپنی جنگجویانہ بہادری کے گُن گاتے ہیں
اور تتلیاں ہم پر یلغار کرتی رہتی ہیں ۔
ہم اپنے قد سے لمبی تلوار کو اسلاف مانتے ہیں
اور ان کا رنگ اپنی زبانوں پر سجا لیتے ہیں
زنگ خوردہ زبانوں اور زمانوں میں زندگی بسر کرنے والوں کا نام
دفتری بابو ہوتا ہے ۔

جاننے والے کا ہر حساب غلط
اور جاننے والے کا ہر حساب درست
زنگ خوردہ زبانیں ہی کہہ سکتی ہیں
اب تو تلوار بنانے والا آہن گر ، یہ سمجھتا ہے
کہ فتح، وہ تحریر کرتا ہے

کشور ناہید

We sing praises of our warlike courage
flies assault us.
A sword taller than ourselves we claim as
our inheritance
Decorating our tongues with our ancestral colours.

Those who live in rusty times amongst rusty tongues
                                            are petty officials.
'The one who's "out" had everything wrong
the one who's "in" has everything right,'
only rusty tongues would say that.
Now even the ironmonger, who makes the sword,
                                                  assumes
it is he who writes victory.

                                              KISHWAR NAHEED

سنسر شپ

جن زمانوں میں کیمرہ ظلم کو ہمیشہ کے لئے
مجسم نہیں کر سکتا تھا
تمہیں ان زمانوں تک ہی
ظلم کو بہادری کا نام دینے کی تاریخ لکھنی چاہئے تھی ۔
آج سلولائیڈ پہ منتقل منظروں کو دیکھ کر اندازہ ہوتا ہے
کہ پہاڑی ڈھلوانوں پہ جیڑوں سے ٹوٹتے درختوں کی آواز اور
منظر نامہ کیسا ہوتا ہے ۔
چاہے تم خوش ہو یا افسردہ
سانس تو لیتے ہو ۔
آنکھیں کھولنے یا بند کرنے سے
ذہن پہ نقش ، منظر نہیں بدلتا ہے
دریا میں کھڑے درخت کا تنا
لکڑی کا ہی رہتا ہے
مگر مچھ نہیں بنتا ہے ۔
ہم کب سے کہانیوں کی چھتوں پر چڑھے یہ سوچ رہے ہیں
کہ یہ شہر ہمارا ہے

Censorship

In those times when the camera could not freeze
                                        tyranny for ever
only until those times
should you have written
that history
which describes tyranny as valour.

Today, gazing at scenes
transferred on celluloid,
one can gauge
what the scene is like
and the sound
when trees are uprooted from the hillsides.

Whether you are happy or sad
you must breathe
Whether your eyes are open or closed
the scene, its imprint on the mind,
does not change.

The tree that stands in the river
always remains wooden
cannot become a crocodile.

For a long time now,
we have stood
on the rooftops of stories
believing this city is ours

بنیاد کی دیواروں کی زمین بیٹھ گئی ہے
مگر اب تک ہم کہاں بنیوں کی چھتوں پہ چڑھے
پچھلی دو پہروں کی اجڑی گلیوں کی ٹوٹی اینٹوں کی
چوڑی دراڑوں کو زندگی سمجھ رہے ہیں ۔

کشور ناہید

The earth beneath the foundations has sunk
but even now we stand
on the rooftops of stories
assuming life to be
the insipid afternoon's wasted alleyways
with their shattered bricks
and gaping fissures.

KISHWAR NAHEED

خود کلامی

مجھے سزا دو
کہ میں نے اپنے لہو سے تعبیرِ خواب لکھی
جنوں بریدہ کتاب لکھی
مجھے سزا دو
کہ میں نے تقدیسِ خوابِ فردا میں جاں گزاری
بہ لطفِ شب زادگاں گزاری
مجھے سزا دو
کہ میں نے قاتل کو وصفِ تیغ و علم سکھایا
سروں کو او ج قلم سکھایا
مجھے سزا دو
کہ میں عدو کی صلیب کی محتسب رہی ہوں
ہوا کی زد پہ جلے چراغوں کی روشنی ہوں
مجھے سزا دو
کہ میں نے دوشیزگیِ کو سودائے شب گماں سے رہائی دی تھی
گھروں کے بجھتے دیوں کو شانِ خدائی دی تھی
مجھے سزا دو
کہ میں جیوں تو تمہاری دستار گر نہ جائے
مجھے سزا دو
کہ میرے بیٹوں کے ہاتھ اٹھے تو تم نہ ہو گے
کہ ایک بھی تیغِ حرفِ قوس سے نکلے تو تم نہ ہو گے

۵۴

Talking to Myself

Punish me
for I have written the significance of the dream
in my own blood
written a book ridden with an obsession
Punish me
for I have spent my life sanctifying the dream of the
                                                           future
spent it enduring the tribulations of the night
Punish me
for I have imparted knowledge and the skills of the
                                         sword to the murderer
and demonstrated the power of the pen to the mind
Punish me
for I have been the challenger of the crucifix of hatred
I'm the glow of torches which burn against the wind
Punish me
for I have freed womanhood from the insanity of the
                                             deluded night
Punish me
for if I live you might lose face
Punish me
for if my sons raise their hands you will meet your end
If only one sword unsheaths itself to speak you will
                                             meet your end

مجھے سزا دو
کہ میں تو ہر سانس میں نئی زندگی کی خوگر
حیات و بعدِ حیات بھی زندہ تر رہوں گی
مجھے سزا دو
کہ پھر تمہاری سزا کی میعاد ختم ہوگی

کشورناہید

Punish me
for I love the new life with every breath
I shall live my life and shall doubly live beyond my life
Punish me for then the sentence of your punishment
                                            will end.

                              KISHWAR NAHEED

اَنٹی کلاک وائز

میری آنکھیں، تمہارے تلووں سے بھی بن جائیں
تو بھی تمہیں یہ خوف نہیں چھوڑے گا
کہیں دیکھ تو نہیں سکتی
جسموں اور فقروں کو
خوشبو کی طرح محسوس تو کر سکتی ہوں
میری ناک اپنے تحفظ کی خاطر
تمہارے سامنے رگڑ رگڑ کر
بے نشان بھی ہو جائے
تو بھی تمہیں یہ خوف نہیں چھوڑے گا
کہیں سونگھ تو نہیں سکتی
مگر کچھ بول تو سکتی ہوں
مرے ہونٹ تمہاری مجازیت کے گن
گا گا کر
خشک اور بے روح ہو بھی جائیں
تو بھی تمہیں یہ خوف نہیں چھوڑے گا
کہیں بول تو نہیں سکتی
مگر چل تو سکتی ہوں
مرے پیروں میں زوجیت
اور شرم و حیا کی بیڑیاں ڈال کر
مجھے مفلوج کرکے بھی
تمہیں یہ خوف نہیں چھوڑے گا
کہیں چل تو نہیں سکتی

Anticlockwise

Even if my eyes become the soles of your feet
even so, the fear will not leave you
that though I cannot see
I can feel bodies and sentences
like a fragrance.

Even if, for my own safety,
I rub my nose in the dirt till it becomes invisible
even so, this fear will not leave you
that though I cannot smell
I can still say something.

Even if my lips, singing praises of your godliness
become dry and soulless
even so, this fear will not leave you
that though I cannot speak
I can still walk.

Even after you have tied the chains of domesticity,
shame and modesty around my feet
even after you have paralysed me
this fear will not leave you
that even though I cannot walk
I can still think.

مگر سوچ تو سکتی ہوں
آزاد رہنے، زندہ رہنے
اور میرے سوچنے کا خوف
تمہیں کن کن بلاؤں میں گرفتار کرے گا

کشور ناہید

Your fear
of my being free, being alive
and able to think
might lead you, who knows, into what travails.

                                  KISHWAR NAHEED

سرد ملکوں کے آقاؤں کے نام

میرا ملک گرم ہے
میرے ہاتھوں کی تپش کا سبب شاید یہی ہے ۔
میرا ملک گرم ہے
میرے پیروں کے جلنے کا سبب شاید یہی ہے ۔
میرا ملک گرم ہے
میرے بدن پہ آبلوں کا سبب شاید یہی ہے ۔
میرا ملک گرم ہے
میرے گھر کی چھت پگھل کر گر جانے کا سبب شاید یہی ہے ۔
میرا ملک گرم ہے
میری دیواروں کے جھلسا دینے کے رویئے کا سبب شاید یہی ہے ۔
میرا ملک گرم ہے
میرے بچوں کے پیاسے رکھے جانے کا سبب شاید یہی ہے ۔
میرا ملک گرم ہے
میرے بے لباس رکھے جانے کا سبب شاید یہی ہے ۔
میرا ملک گرم ہے
شاید اسی لئے نہ برستے بادلوں کے آنے کا پتہ چلتا ہے ۔
اور نہ سیلابوں کے گزر جانے کا
کہ میری فصلوں کے اجاڑنے کو
کبھی مہاجن کبھی جنگلی جانور ، کبھی آفتیں
اور کبھی خود ساختہ آقا آن دھمکتے ہیں ۔
مجھے اپنے گرم ملک سے نفرت کرنا مت سکھاؤ
مجھے ان آنگنوں میں اپنے گیلے کپڑے سکھانے دو
مجھے اس کے کھلیانوں میں سونا اگانے دو

To the Masters of Countries with a Cold Climate

My country is torrid
maybe that is why my hands feel warm
My country is torrid
maybe that is why my feet burn
My country is torrid
maybe that is why there are boils on my body
My country is torrid
maybe that is why the roof of my house melted and
                                            caved in.

My country is torrid
maybe that is why my children are kept thirsty
My country is torrid
maybe that is why I am kept unclothed.

My country is torrid
maybe that is why one neither knows of clouds which
                                        bring rainfall
nor of floods that destroy.
And to wreck my harvests, sometimes moneylenders,
        sometimes wild beasts, sometimes calamities
and sometimes self-styled masters arrive.

Don't teach me to hate my torrid country
Let me dry my wet clothes in these courtyards
let me plant gold in its fields

مجھے اس کے دریاؤں سے پیاس بجھانے دو
مجھے اس کے درختوں کی چھاؤں میں سانس لینے دو
مجھے اس دھول کو پہننے اور مسافتوں کو اوڑھنے دو
مجھے لبے ہوتے سایوں کی چھاؤں نہیں چاہیے
مجھے تو نکلتے سورج کی شعاعوں کی حمایت حاصل ہے
سورج اپنی توانائی میرے ملک میں ارزاں کرتا ہے

کشور ناہید

let me quench my thirst at its rivers
let me rest beneath the shade of its trees
let me wear its dust and wrap its distances around me.
I don't want the shade of lengthening shadows
I have the support of the rays of the rising sun.
The sun has made its energy accessible for my country
the sun and I
the sun and you
cannot walk side by side.
The sun has chosen *me* for company.

           KISHWAR NAHEED

رجم

"ابنِ عمر سے روایت ہے کہ جب بدکاری کرنے والے جوڑے کو سنگسار کیا گیا تو مرد عورت پر جھک جھک جاتا اور اسے پتھروں سے بچاتا"

پاگل تن میں کیوں بستی ہے
یہ وحشی ، تاریک آرزو
بہت قدیم اداس آرزو
تاریکی میں چھپ جانے کی
اک لمحے کو
اک لمحے کو
رب قہار! یہ معجزہ کیا ہے!
تیرا خلق کیا ہوا آدم
لذتِ سنگ کا کیوں خواہاں ہے
اس کی سحر زدہ چیخوں میں
یک برزخ کا نغمہ ہے
کیا یہی بدن کے زخم کی لذت
بے تابی سے یوں رقصاں ہے
بر بن مو سے سرخ و سیاہ لہو کا دریا ابل پڑا ہے۔

فہمیدہ ریاض

*Stoning**

'According to a story attributed to Ibn-e-Omer, when an adulterous couple was being stoned the man kept leaning over the woman to shield her from the stones.'

Why does the crazed body harbour
This barbaric desire
Very ancient sad desire
To enter the darkness
For an instant
For an instant?

What a miracle, O God of wrath,
That Adam created by you
Should seek to taste this death by stoning.
What limbo lends melody to his enchanted screams?
What was the ecstasy of the wound
Which dances so restlessly
While from every pore erupts a black and red river of blood.

FAHMIDA RIAZ

*Please see introduction: Hudood Ordinance.

سورۃ یاسین

یہ آخر شب کا سناٹا!
اس نیم اندھیرے رستے پر
جلدی میں قدم بڑھاتی ہوئی
میں ایک اکیلی عورت ہوں
بڑی دیر سے میرے تعاقب میں
اک چاپ ہے جو چلی آتی ہے
گھر۔۔۔۔!
میرا گھر۔۔۔!
میں اپنے گھر کیسے پہنچوں
سوکھے حلقوم اور شبہتے دل سے سوچتی ہوں
شاید میں رستہ بھول گئی
یہ راہ تو میری راہ نہیں
اس راہ سے میں کب گزری تھی
سب گلیوں پر یہاں نام لکھے
اس گلی پہ کوئی نام نہیں
اور دور دور تک دم سادھے
یہ سارے گھر انجانے ہیں
لو پچھلے چاند کا ٹکڑا بھی
کالے پتوں میں ڈوب گیا
اب کچھ بھی نہیں
بس میرے منہ میں خوف سے بھاری اور مفلوج یہ زباں ہے
یا
تلووں سے اوپر چڑھتی ہوئی
میرے انگ انگ میں رچی ہوئی
اک خنکی ہے

فہمیدہ ریاض

Surah-e-Yaaseen*

Late at night, this eerie silence!
In this dimly dark pathway,
with hurridly advancing footsteps,
I am a lone woman.
For a long time now I have heard
the sound of footsteps following me.
Home!
My home!
How do I get to my home?
With parched throat and a sinking heart I think.
Perhaps I have forgotten my way,
this way is not my way,
all the alleyways are marked here
that alley has no name
and for miles and miles, holding their breath,
all these houses are unfamiliar.
There! Even the fragmented yellow moon
has drowned in the dark leaves.
Now there is nothing
Except in my mouth, heavy with fear and paralysed,
                              my tongue.
Or, rising upwards, through the soles of my feet,
suffusing each and every pore of my body,
a certain dampness.

                                      FAHMIDA RIAZ

*A Muslim prayer equivalent to the Lord's Prayer

اے والی و ربّ کون و مکاں

ڈوب گئی خاموشی میں مغرب کی اذاں
کیسا سکوت ہے ، والی و ربّ کون و مکاں
الحمدللہ ربّ العالمین
سب تعریف خدا کی ہے ، جو ہے بہت عظیم
بارش سے نکھرا نکھرا شفاف فلک
نیلا نیلا حد نظر تک پھیلا ہے
سبزے کی مخمل سے ڈھکی ہے نرم زمین
الحمدللہ ربّ العالمین
سب تعریف خدا کی ہے ، جو ہے بہت عظیم
کیسی سوچ نے میرے دل میں چٹکی لی
کیسے دھیان سے میری آنکھیں بھر آئیں
سینے میں کیوں سناٹا سا چھایا ہے
یہ میرے سجدے میں تذبذب کیسا ہے
لب پہ دعائیں آکے بنیں کیوں بے معنی
جیسے میرا اندر ہو سنسان اجاڑ
کوئی تو آئے کوئی تو آکر دستک دے
کیسے کھولوں اپنے دل کے بند کواڑ

فہمیدہ ریاض

O God of Heaven and Earth

At twilight the call to prayer sinks into silence
What stillness, O God of Heaven and Earth!

'Praised be God, the God of all the worlds
All praise to God who is very great.'

The rainwashed sparkling sky
Spreads blue as far as the eye can see.
The soft earth is clad in velvety green.
'Praised be God, the God of all the worlds
All praise to God who is very great.'

What thought is this which wrings my heart
What realisation fills my eyes with tears
Why is this eerie silence in my bosom
What is this hesitation in my worship?
Why do my prayers become meaningless on my lips?
As if all within me were desolate and uninhabited.
If only someone would come, if only someone would
                                    come and knock
How can I open the locked doors of my heart?

FAHMIDA RIAZ

لاؤ، ہاتھ اپنا لاؤ ذرا

لاؤ، ہاتھ اپنا لاؤ ذرا
چھو کے میرا بدن
اپنے بچے کے دل کا دھڑکنا سنو
ناف کے اس طرف
اس کی جنبش کو محسوس کرتے ہو تم؟
بس یہیں چھوڑ دو
تھوڑی دیر اور اس ہاتھ کو میرے ٹھنڈے بدن پر یہیں پڑے رہنے دو
میرے بے کل نفس کو قرار آ گیا
میرے عیسیٰ میرے درد کے چارہ گر
میرا ہر مو نے تن
اس ہتھیلی سے تسکین پانے لگا
اس ہتھیلی کے نیچے مرا لال کروٹ سی لینے لگا
انگلیوں سے بدن اس کا پہچان لو
تم اسے جان لو
چومنے دو مجھے اپنی یہ انگلیاں
ان کی ہر پور کو چومنے دو مجھے
ناخنوں کو لبوں سے لگا لوں ذرا
اس ہتھیلی میں منہ تو چھپا لوں ذرا
پھول لاگتی ہوئی یہ ہری انگلیاں
میری آنکھوں سے آنسو بلکتے ہوئے
ان سے سینچوں گی میں
پھول لاگتی ہوئی انگلیوں کی جڑیں۔ چومنے دو مجھے
اپنے بال ۰ اپنے ماتھے کا چاند، اپنے لب
یہ چمکتی ہوئی کالی آنکھیں

۲

Come, Give Me Your Hand.

Come, give me your hand
touch my body
and listen to the beating of your child's heart
On that side of the navel
can you feel it stirring?

Leave it here
for a little while longer, this hand on my cold body
My restless being has found tranquillity
My Jesus, the healer of my pain
every pore of my body
finds relief through this palm
Beneath this palm my precious child seems to turn

Let your fingers know its body
get to know it
let me kiss these fingers of yours
let me kiss each and every fingertip
let me touch your nails with my lips
let me hide my face in this palm for a bit
these green fingers which bring flowers
With the tears which bubble up in my eyes
I shall tend these
the roots of these fingers which bring flowers
let me kiss them
the hair, the moon of your forehead, your lips
these shining black eyes,

مرے کا پنپتے ہونٹ ، مری چھلکتی ہوئی آنکھ کو دیکھ کر کتنی حیران ہیں
تم کو معلوم کیا ۔ تم کو معلوم کیا
تم نے جانے مجھے کیا سے کیا کر دیا
میرے اندر اندھیرے کا اک سیپ تھا
یا کراں تا کراں ایک انمٹ خلا
یوں ہی بھرتی تھی میں
ظلمت کے ذائقے کو ترستی ہوئی
دل میں آنسو بھرے ، سب پہ ہنستی ہوئی
تم نے اندر میرا اس طرح بھر دیا
پھوٹتی ہے مرے جسم سے روشنی
سب مقدس کتابیں جو نازل ہوئیں
سب پیمبر جو اب تک اتارے گئے
سب فرشتے کہ ہیں بادلوں سے پرے
رنگ، سنگیت، سُر، پھول، کلیاں، شجر
صبحدم پیڑ کی جھومتی ڈالیاں
ان کے مفہوم جو مجھی بتائے گئے
خاک پر بسنے والے بشر کو مسرت کے جتنے بھی نغمے سنائے گئے
سب رشی، سب منی، انبیاء اولیا
خیر کے دیوتا ، حسن ، نیکی ، خدا ۔۔۔
آج سب پر مجھے
اعتبار آگیا ۔ اعتبار آگیا

فہمیدہ ریاض

so amazed at my trembling lips and my brimming eye.
What do you know? What do you know of
how you have transformed me?
Within me was a haunting darkness
a limitless, endless space
I wandered around aimlessly
longing for a taste of life
with tears filling my heart, I laughed at everyone
you filled my womb so
that light pours forth from my body.

All the sacred texts that ever descended
all the prophets sent to earth
all the angels beyond the clouds
colour, music, melody, flowers, buds and trees
at dawn the swaying branches of the trees
the meanings which were assigned to all of these
All the songs of joy which have been sung to earthly beings
all the saints, all the fakirs, all the prophets, all the visionaries
the gods of well-being, beauty, goodness, God –
in all of them today
I have come to believe, I have come to believe.

FAHMIDA RIAZ

آڈن کے نام

یہ سچ ہے میرے فلسفی
میرے شاعر
وہ وقت آ گیا ہے
کہ دنیا کے بوڑھے فریبی معلّم کا جبّہ پکڑ کر
ننے لوگ کہہ دیں
کتابیں بدل دو!
یہ جھوٹی کتابیں
جو ہم کو پڑھاتے چلے آ رہے ہیں
حقیقت کے رخ سے
یہ بے معنی فرسودہ لفظوں کے پردے ہٹا دو
جلا دو
کتابیں جو ہم نے پڑھی ہیں
جلا دو
کتابیں جو کہتی ہیں دنیا میں حق جیتتا ہے
یہ سب کذب و بیہودہ گوئی مٹا دو
یہ سب کچھ غلط ہے
کہ ہم جانتے ہیں
کہ جھوٹ اور سچ میں ہمیشہ ہوئی جنگ
اور
جھوٹ جیتا ہے
کہ نفرت امر ہے
کہ طاقت ہے بر حق
کہ سچ ہارتا ہے
کہ شیطان نیکی کے احمق خدا سے بڑا ہے

فہمیدہ ریاض

To Auden

'Tis true, my philosopher,
My poet.
Those times are here
When pulling at the gown of
The old deceitful scholar of the world
The young would demand:
Change our texts
These lying books
That have been taught for so long
Remove from the visage of truth
The veils of worn and meaningless words
Burn them
Those books that we have read
Burn them
The books that claim that in this world truth always
                                                                  wins

Erase these lies, these vulgarisms
They are all wrong
We know that Truth and Falsehood have always been
                                                                  at war.
And
Falsehood wins
That hatred lives for ever
That might is right
That Truth is defeated
That Satan is mightier than the stupid God of virtue.

                                                    FAHMIDA RIAZ

باکرہ

آسمان تپتے ہوئے لوہے کی مانند سفید
ریگ سوکھی ہوئی پیاسی کی زبان کے مانند
پیاس حلقوم میں ہے، جسم میں ہے، جان میں ہے
سر بہ زانو ہوں ۔ تپتے ہوئے ریگستاں میں
تیری سرکار میں لے آئی ہوں یہ وحشی ذبیح!
مجھ پہ لازم تھی جو قربانی وہ میں نے کر دی
اس کی ابلی ہوئی آنکھوں میں ابھی تک ہے چمک
اور سیہ بال ہیں بھیگے ہونے خوں سے اب تک
تیرا فرمان یہ تھا اس پہ کوئی داغ نہ ہو
سو یہ بے عیب اچھوتا بھی تھا ان دیکھا بھی

بے کراں ریگ میں سب گرم لہو جذب ہوا
دیکھ چادر پہ مری ثبت ہے اس کا دھبا
اے خداوند کبیر
اے جبّار!
متکبّر و جلیل!
ہاں ترے نام پڑھے اور کیا ذبیح اسے
اب کوئی پارہ ابر آئے، کہیں سایہ ہو
اے خداوندِ عظیم
باد تسکیں! کہ نفس آگ بنا جاتا ہے!
قطرۂ آب کہ جاں لب پہ چلی آئی ہے

فہمیدہ ریاض

Virgin

The sky glows white like heated iron
The sand is dry as a parched thirsty tongue
Thirsty is the throat, the body, life itself.

My head bowed, I sit in the scalding desert
I have brought under your command this sacrificial
                                                   animal!
The sacrifice which was obligatory, I have made.
There is still a glow in its bulging eyes
Its black hair is still soaked with blood
You had ordained that it should be unmarked
So it was, faultless, untouched and unseen too.
The warm blood absorbs in the endless sands
Look, it has stamped a stain on my *chadur*.
O Great God
O Imperious One
O Proud and Angry One
Yes, I read your names and slaughtered it
Now let a shred of cloud come, let there be shade
                                              somewhere
O Great God
A breath of solace, for the soul itself is on fire!
A drop of water, for life is edging towards its end.

                                                  FAHMIDA RIAZ

کوتوال بیٹھا ہے

کوتوال بیٹھا ہے
کیا بیاں دیں اس کو
(جان جیسے تڑپی ہے
کچھ عیاں نہ ہو پائے
وہ گزر گئی دل پر
جو بیاں نہ ہو پائے)

لو بیان دیتے ہیں
ہاں لکھو کہ سب سچ ہے
سب درست الزامات
اپنا جرم ثابت ہے
جو کیا بہت کم تھا
صرف یہ ندامت ہے
کاش وقت پھر آئے
حق ادا ہوا ہے
کب۔

یہ کرو اضافہ اب
جب تک ہے دم میں دم
پھر وہی کریں گے ہم
ہو سکا تو کچھ بڑھ کر
پھر وہ حرف لکھیں گے
تیرہ زاد ہر آدم
کانپ اٹھے جسے پڑھ کر

۱۰

*The Interrogator**

The Interrogator is waiting –
What should be our statement?
>Our suffering
>Is hard to reveal
>What the heart has
>>endured
>Impossible to recount.

Here is my statement then:
So take note, this is all true.
All the allegations are true
my crime is proven
What I did was too little, though
that is my only regret
I hope for another chance
I owed more than I have paid as yet.
To all that, add this too:
So long as I breathe
I shall do it again

If possible I shall do it better
We shall write that word again
To make every dictator equipped with his armoury
Tremble upon reading that word
We shall play that tune again
To make every victim of oppression,
with hands folded,
Dance to its rhythm.

*The word used in Urdu implies a police officer who is hostile/villainous

پھر وہ گیت چھیڑیں گے

لبستہ دست ہر مظلوم
جھوم اٹھے جسے گا کر
چیتھڑا ہے یہ قانون!
باغیوں کے قدموں کی
اس بے دھول جھاڑیں گے
آمری نحوست ہے
یہ نظام احکامات
بیچ چوک پھاڑیں گے

وقت آنے والا ہے
احتساب ہم لیں گے
جب حساب ہم لیں گے
پھر جواب دینے کو
تم مگر کہاں ہو گے

خار و خس سے کم تر ہو
راستے کے کنکر ہو
جس نے راہ گھیری ہے

وہ تمہارا آقا ہے
ہم نے دل میں ٹھانی ہے
راہ صاف کر دیں گے
تم ، کہ صرف نوکر ہو
تم کو معاف کر دیں گے

فہمیدہ ریاض

                    This law is a rag
                    Worthy of the dust
                    Off the rebels' feet
                    Dictatorship a curse
                    This government of
                    Ordinances
                    We shall shred
                    in a public square.
The time is coming
for accountability
When they must account for it all
But then, to answer for this,
Where would you be?
                    Less than a thorn, less
                    than dust
                    You are but a pebble by
                    the wayside
                    Which obstructs the path
                    He is your master
We have now decided to clear the way
You who are only his instrument
You, we shall forgive.

                                          FAHMIDA RIAZ

تصویر

مرے دل کے نہاں خانے میں اک تصویر ہے میری
خدا جانے اسے اُس نے بنایا ، کب بنایا تھا
یہ پوشیدہ ہے میرے دوستوں سے اور مجھ سے بھی
کبھی بھولے سے لیکن میں اسے گر دیکھ لیتی ہوں
اسے خود سے ملاؤں تو مرا دل کانپ جاتا ہے

فہمیدہ ریاض

Image

Deep in the recesses of my heart hangs a picture of
                                              myself
God knows who painted it and when
There it remains hidden from me and my friends
but if ever I glimpse it, even by accident,
My heart shudders at the comparison with myself.

                                        FAHMIDA RIAZ

خانہ تلاشی

کوتوال :-
"دیکھو بی بی ، یہ پروانہ خانہ تلاشی کا لایا ہوں
نفری سائقہ ہے ۔ لیکن اس کو گلی میں دور ہٹا آیا ہوں
سوچا ،میں خود ہی کافی ہوں
ہے درکار ہمیں اک مضموں
رسوائی سے کیا حاصل ہے خود ہی آپ نکال کے لا دیں
ورنہ گھر میں کہاں چھپا ہے ؟ سیدھی طرح ہمیں دکھلا دیں" ۔
اپنے گھر کو اس طرح پہلے کبھی دیکھا نہ تھا
دل دھڑکتا سن رہی ہوں مَیں درو دیوار میں
سنگ و آہن کی وریدوں سے ٹپکتا ہے لہو
گرم سانسیں ، جاگتی آنکھیں ، کھلے لب چار سو
مجھ سے سرگوشی میں پھر اک بار دہراتے ہوئے
سات جنموں کا بندھا پیہا وطن کی خاک سے
چار دیواریں مری دھرتی تری آغوش میں
عافیت کی چار گھڑیاں مجھ پہ تیرا قرض ہیں
کتنے تہہ خانے ابھر آئے نظر کے سامنے
کتنے امکاں ہیں کہ جن کے آج مجھ پر در کھلے
کھل گئیں قدموں تلے میری مرادوں کی سرنگ
جس کی دیواروں پہ روشن زندگی کے سات رنگ

Search Warrant

The Interrogator:
'Look here, *Bibi**, here is the search warrant;
The contingent were with me,
but I left them round the corner
I thought, I can manage on my own.
We are looking for a piece of writing.
What's the point in making a scene?
Why don't you find it,
Fetch it yourself?
Or else, where it lies, hidden in the house,
Show us, without a fuss, yourself.'

Never have I seen my house in this light before
I can hear a heartbeat throb in its very walls
Blood drips from the veins of stones and steel
Warm breaths, wakeful eyes, parted lips surround me
Repeat their whisper to me once again
Of the promised eternal bond with my country
My four walls, dear land, nestle in your arms
the few moments of refuge I had, I owe you.
Countless cellars arise before my eyes
Countless possibilities open their doors for me
Beneath my feet opens the tunnel of my hopes
all seven colours of life glowing on its walls.

*An Urdu equivalent for 'ladies' which is also a respectful form of address used for the Prophet's wives and daughters or for saints.

اب وضیں شہر پر ہوں گے ننے مضمون رقم
اے گزرتے پل! تیری پامال حرمت کی قسم
جس گلی میں میرا گھر ہے، سرخ اس کی دھول ہے
اس دریچے سے پرے لالہ کا کھلتا پھول ہے
اس قدر خطرے کا باعث ایک ماضی کی کتاب!
دیکھ یہ چلمن ہٹا کر میرے مستقبل کا خواب!

فہمیدہ ریاض

New words will be inscribed now on the walls of this city
O passing moment! I swear by your desecrated honour
Red is the dust around my house
Beyond this window blooms a red flower.

All these tribulations I endure
over a book buried in my past?

Look beyond the curtains instead
At the dreams my future holds!

FAHMIDA RIAZ

چادر اور دیواری

حضور میں اس سیاہ چادر کا کیا کروں گی
یہ آپ کیوں مجھ کو بخشتے ہیں، بصد عنایت!

نہ سوگ میں ہوں کہ اس کو اوڑھوں
غم و الم خلق کو دکھاؤں
نہ روگ ہوں میں کہ اس کی تاریکیوں میں خفت سے ڈوب جاؤں
نہیں گنہگار ہوں نہ مجرم
کہ اس سیاہی کی مہر اپنی جبیں پہ ہر حال میں لگاؤں
اگر نہ گستاخ مجھ کو سمجھیں

اگر میں جان کی امان پاؤں
تو دست بستہ کروں گزارش
کہ بندہ پرور!
حضور کے حجرۂ معطر میں ایک لاشہ پڑا ہوا ہے
نہ جانے کب کا گلا سڑا ہے
یہ آپ سے رحم چاہتا ہے
حضور اتنا کرم تو کیجئے
سیاہ چادر مجھے نہ دیجئے
سیاہ چادر سے اپنے حجرہ کی بے کفن لاش ڈھانپ دیجئے
کہ اس سے پھوٹی ہے جو عفونت
وہ کوچے کوچے میں ہانپتی ہے
وہ سر پٹختی ہے جھروکوں پر
برہنگی اپنی ڈھانکتی ہے
سنیں ذرا دلخراش چیخیں

Chadur and Diwari

Sire! What use is this black *chadur* to me?
A thousand mercies, why do you reward me with this?

I am not in mourning that I should wear this
To flag my grief to the world
I am not a disease that needs to be drowned in secret darkness
I am not a sinner, nor a criminal,
That I should stamp my forehead with its darkness
If you will not consider me too impudent
If you promise that you will spare my life
I beg to submit in all humility,
O Master of Men!
In Your Highness' fragrant chambers
lies a dead body
Who knows how long it has been rotting?
It seeks pity from you

Sire, do be so kind
Do not give me this black *chadur*
With this black *chadur* cover the shroudless body lying in your chamber
For the stench that emanates from that body
Walks huffed and breathless in every alleyway
Bangs her head on every door frame
Covering her nakedness
Listen to her heart-rending screams

بنارسی ہیں عجب بیوے
جو چادروں میں بھی ہیں برہنہ
یہ کون ہیں؟ جانتے تو ہوں گے
حضور پہچانتے تو ہوں گے
یہ لونڈیاں ہیں !
کہ یرغمالی حلالِ شب بھر رہیں ۔
دمِ صبح در بدر ہیں
یہ باندیاں ہیں ۔

حضو کے لفظۂ مبارک کے لفظ و رش سے معتبر ہیں
یہ بیبیاں ہیں !
کہ زوجگی کا خراج دینے
قطار اندر قطار باری کی منتظر ہیں ۔

یہ بچیاں ہیں !
کہ جن کے سر پر پھرا جو حضرت کا دستِ شفقت

تو کم سنی کے لہو سے ریشِ سپید رنگین ہو گئی ہے
حضور کے حجلۂ معطر میں زندگی خون رو گئی ہے
پڑا ہوا ہے جہاں یہ لاشہ
طویل صدیوں سے قتلِ انسانیت کا یہ خوں چکاں تماشا
اب اس تماشے کو ختم کیجئے
حضور اب اس کو ڈھانپ دیجئے !
سیاہ چادر تو بن چکی ہے مری نہیں آپ کی ضرورت

۹۲

Which raise strange spectres
That remain naked in spite of their *chadurs*.

Who are they? YOU must know them, Sire,
Your Highness must recognise them
These are the handmaidens
The hostages who are *halal* for the night
With the breath of morning they become homeless
they are the slaves who are beyond
the half-share of inheritance for your Highness'
offspring

These are the *Bibis**
Who wait to fulfil their vows of marriage
In turn, as they stand, row upon row.
They are the maidens,
On whose heads Your Highness laid a hand of
paternal affection,
Making the blood of their innocent youth stain the
whiteness of your beard with red.
In your fragrant chamber, tears of blood,
Life itself has shed
Where this carcass has lain
For long centuries – this bloody spectacle of the
murder of humanity

Bring this show to an end now,
Sire, cover it up now
Not I, but *you* need this *chadur* now

---

* See footnote on p. 87.

کہ اس زمیں پر وجود میرا نہیں فقط اک نشانِ شہوت
حیات کی شاہراہ پر جگمگا رہی ہے مری ذہانت
زمیں کے رخ پر جو ہے پسینہ تو جھلملاتی ہے میری محنت
یہ چار دیواریاں ، یہ چادر ، گلی سڑی لاش کو مبارک
کھلی فضاؤں میں باد باں کھول کر بڑھے گا مرا سفینہ
میں آدم نوح کی ہم سفر ہوں
کہ جس نے جیتی مری بجر و سا بھری رفاقت !

فہمیدہ ریاض

For my person is not merely a symbol of your lust
Across the highways of life glows my intelligence
If a bead of sweat sparkles on earth's brow it is my
diligence.

These four walls, this *chadur* I wish upon the rotting
carcass
In the open air, her sails flapping, my ship races ahead

I am the companion of the new Adam
Who has earned my self-assured love.

FAHMIDA RIAZ

وہ اک زن ناپاک ہے

وہ اک زن ناپاک ہے
بہتے لہو کی قید میں
گردش میں ماہ و ساں کی
دہکی ہوس کی آگ میں
اپنی طلب کی چاہ میں
زائیدۂ ابلیس تھی
چل دی اسی کی راہ میں
اس منزلِ موہوم کو
جس کا نشاں پیدا نہیں
سنگم وہ نور و نار کا
جس کا پتا ملتا نہیں
ابلے لہو کے جوش سے
پستان اس کے پھٹ چکے
ہر نوکِ خارِ راہ سے
بندِ لحم سب کٹ چکے
اس کے بدن کی شرم پر
تقدیس کا سایہ نہیں

لیکن خدائے بجبروبر
ایسا کبھی دیکھا نہیں
فرمان تیرے سب روا
ہاں اس زن ناپاک کے
لب پر نہیں کوئی دعا
سر میں کوئی سجدہ نہیں

فہمیدہ ریاض

She Is a Woman Impure

She is a woman impure
imprisoned by her flowing blood
in a cycle of months and years.
Consumed by her fiery lust,
in search of her own desire,
this mistress of the devil
followed his footsteps
into a destination obscure
unmarked, unmapped before,
that union of light and fire
impossible to find.

In the heat of her simmering passion
her breasts have ripped
By each thorn on the wayside
every membrane of her body ripped.
No veil of shame conceals her body
No trace it bears of sanctity.

But, O Ruler of lands and oceans,
Who has seen this before?
Everywhere your command is supreme
Except over this woman impure
No prayer crosses her lips
No humility touches her brow.

                          FAHMIDA RIAZ

اقلیما

اقلیما
جو ہابیل کی قابیل کی ماں جائی ہے
ماں جائی
مگر مختلف
مختلف بیچ میں رانوں کے
اور پستانوں کے ابھار میں
اور اپنے پیٹ کے اندر
اور کوکھ میں
ان سب کی قسمت کیوں ہے
اک فربہ بھیڑ کے بچے کی قربانی
وہ اپنے بدن کی قیدی
تپتی ہوئی دھوپ میں جلتے
ٹیلے پر کھڑی ہوئی ہے
پتھر پر نقش بنی ہے
اس نقش کو غور سے دیکھو
لمبی رانوں سے اوپر
ابھرے پستانوں سے اوپر
پیچیدہ کوکھ سے اوپر
اقلیما کا سر بھی ہے
اللہ کبھی اقلیما سے بھی کلام کرے
اور کچھ پوچھے!

فہمیدہ ریاض

Akleema

Akleema*,
the sister of Cain and Abel,
is born of the same mother
but she is different.
Different between her thighs
And in the bulge of her breasts
Different in her gut
and inside her womb
Why is the fate of all of these
the sacrifice of a fatted lamb?

Imprisoned by her own body
burning in the scalding sun
She stands on a hilltop
like a mark etched on stone
Look at this mark carefully
above the long thighs
above the high breasts
above the tangled womb
Akleema has a head too
Let God speak to Akleema some time
And ask her something.

FAHMIDA RIAZ

*A version of the legend claims that the brothers fought over their sister Akleema's hand.

ایک عورت کی ہنسی

پتھریلے کوہسار کے گاتے چشموں میں
گونج رہی ہے اک عورت کی نرم ہنسی
دولت، طاقت اور شہرت، سب کچھ بھی نہیں
اس کے بدن میں چھپی ہے اس کی آزادی
دنیا کے معبد کے نئے بت پتھ کریں
سن نہیں سکتے اس کی لذت کی سسکی
اس بازار میں گوہرِ مال بکاؤ ہے
کوئی خریدے کہ لائے ذرا تسکین اس کی
اک سرشاری جس سے وہ ہی واقف ہے
چاہے بھی تو اس کو نیچ نہیں سکتی
وادی کی آوارہ ہواؤ! آجاؤ
آؤ اور اس کے چہرے پر بوسے دو
اپنے لمبے لمبے بال اڑاتی جائے

فہمیدہ ریاض

The Laughter of a Woman

In the singing springs of stony mountains
Echoes the gentle laughter of a woman
Wealth, power and fame mean nothing
In her body, hidden, lies her freedom
Let the new gods of the earth try as they can
They cannot hear the sob of her ecstasy.
Everything sells in this market-place
save her satisfaction
the ecstasy she alone knows
which she herself cannot sell

Come you wild winds of the valley
Come and kiss her face

There she goes, her hair billowing in the wind
The daughter of the wind
There she goes, singing with the wind.

FAHMIDA RIAZ

عورت اور نمک

عزت کی بہت سی قسمیں ہیں
گھونگھٹ ۔ تپڑ ۔ گندم
عزت کے تابوت میں قید کی مشینیں ٹھونکی گئی ہیں
گھر سے لے کر فٹ پاتھ تک میک اپ ہمارا نہیں
عزت ہمارے گزارے کی بات ہے
عزت کے نیزے سے ہمیں داغا جاتا ہے
عزت کی کہانی ہماری زباں سے شروع ہوتی ہے
کوئی رات ہمارا نمک چکھ لے
تو ایک زندگی ہمیں بے ذائقہ روٹی کہا جاتا ہے
یہ کیسا بازار ہے
کہ رنگ ساز ہی پھیکا پڑا ہے
خلا کی بھٹی پہ پتنگیں مر رہی ہیں
ہم قید میں بچے جنتی ہوں
جائز اولاد کے لئے زمین کھلنڈری ہونی چاہئے
تم دریس نیچے جنتی ہو اسی لئے آج تمہاری کوئی نسل نہیں
تم جسم کے ایک بند سے پکاری جاتی ہو
تمہاری حیثیت ہیں تو چال رکھ دی گئی ہے
ایک خوبصورت چال
جھوٹی مسکراہٹ تمہارے لبوں پہ تراشی دی گئی ہے
تم صدیوں سے نہیں روئیں

Woman and Salt

There are many types of respectability
the veil, a slap, wheat,
stakes of imprisonment are hammered into the coffin
                                  of respectability

From house to pavement we own nothing
respectability has to do with how we manage
respectability is the spear used to brand us
the selvedge of respectability begins on our tongues
If someone tastes the salt of our bodies at night
for a lifetime we become tasteless bread
Strange market this
where even the dyer has no colours
The kites on the palm of space are dying

I deliver babies in imprisonment
the earth should be playful for legitimate offspring
Because you deliver children in fear today you have no
                                                          pedigree
you are known by the name of one wall of your body

How you conduct yourself has been made central to
                                                          your status
a beautiful gait
a false smile chiselled on your lips
you haven't wept for years

کیا ماں ایسی ہوتی ہے
تمہارے بچے بھیکیے کیوں پڑے ہیں
تم کس کمینے کی ماں ہو
ریپ کی ۔ قید کی ۔ بنے ہوئے جسم کی
یا اینٹوں میں چنی ہوئی بیٹیوں کی
بازاروں میں تمہاری بیٹیاں
اپنے لہو سے بھوک گوندھتی ہیں
اور اپنا گوشت کھاتی ہیں
یہ تمہاری کون سی آنکھیں ہیں
یہ تمہارے گھر کی دیوار کی کون سی چنائی ہے
تم نے میری ہنسی میں ہیں تعارف رکھا
اور اپنے بیٹے کا نام سکہ رائج الوقت
آج تمہاری بیٹی اپنی بیٹیوں سے کہتی ہے
میں اپنی بیٹی کی زبان داغوں گی
لو تھوکتی عورت دہات نہیں
چوڑیوں کی چور نہیں
میدان میرا حوصلہ ہے
انگارہ میری خواہش
ہم سر پہ کفن باندھ کر پیدا ہوئے ہیں
کوئی انگوٹھی پہن کر نہیں
جسے تم چوری کر لو

سارہ شگفتہ

۱۰۴

Is that what a mother is like
Why have your children turned pale
Which tribe of mothers do you belong to
That of rape, imprisonment, or a divided body
or of daughters bricked up alive.
Your daughters in the streets
knead hunger with their own blood
and eat their own flesh.
Which of your eyes are these
How many times has the wall of your house been
                                                      bricked up
You let my daughter be my name
but your son's name is the currency of the time

Today, your daughter tells her own daughters
I shall brand my daughter's tongue
blood-spitting woman is not a metal
is not looking for bangles to steal –
A battleground my courage, a spark my desire

We were born wearing shrouds around our heads
not rings on our fingers
which you might steal.

                                          SARA SHAGUFTA

شیلی بیٹی کے نام

تجھے جب بھی کوئی دکھ دے
اس دکھ کا نام بیٹی رکھنا
جب میرے سفید بال
تیرے گالوں پہ آن ہنسیں، رو لینا
میرے خواب کے دکھ پہ سو لینا
جن کھیتوں کو ابھی اگنا ہے
ان کھیتوں میں
میں دیکھتی ہوں تیری انگیا بھی
لبس پہلی بار ڈری بیٹی
میں کتنی بار ڈری بیٹی
ابھی پیڑوں میں چھپے تیرے کمان ہیں بیٹی
میرا جنم تو ہے بیٹی
اور تیرا جنم تیری بیٹی
تجھے نہلانے کی خواہش میں
میری پوریں خون ٹپکتی ہیں

سارہ شگفتہ

To Daughter, Sheely

Whenever someone gives you a sorrow
name that sorrow, 'daughter'.
When my grey hairs appear
laughing around your cheeks, you can weep
on the sorrow of my dream, you can sleep

Those fields which are yet to grow
in those fields
ı see your brassière too.

I was afraid
but only the first time, daughter.
How many were the times I felt afraid, daughter?

Trees hide the archers who lie in wait for you
You were my birth, daughter,
and your birth, your daughter will be

In the desire to bathe you
my fingertips spit blood.

SARA SHAGUFTA

چاند کتنا تنہا ہے

پنجرے کا سایہ بھی قید ہے
لباس کا سایہ میں ہوتی جا رہی ہوں
میرے ہاتھ دو سروں میں لبس رہتے ہیں
مٹی اکیلی ہو گئی ہے
اکیلا دریا سمندر کیوں گیا
قضیہ کتنا تنہا ہے
روٹھ روٹھ جاتی ہوں مرنے والوں سے
ادر جاگ اٹھتی ہوں آگ میں
گونج رہی ہوں پتھر میں
ڈوب چلی ہوں مٹی میں کونسا پیڑ اگے گا
میرے دکھوں کا نام بچہ ہے
میرے ہاتھوں میں ٹوٹے کھلونے
اور آنکھوں میں السان ہے
بے شمار جسم مجھ سے آنکھیں مانگ رہے ہیں
میں کہاں سے اپنی ابتدا کروں
آسمانوں کی عمر میری عمر سے چھوٹی ہے
پرواز زمین نہیں رکھتی
ہاتھ کس کی آواز ہیں
میرے جھوٹ سمہ لینا
جب جنگل سے پرندوں کو آزاد کر دو
چراغ کو آگ چکھتی ہے
میں ذات کی منڈیر پر پکڑ سے سکھاتی ہوں
میرے فاصلے میں آنکھ ہے

۱۰۸

The Moon Is Quite Alone

The shadow of the cage is imprisoned too
I become the shadow of my apparel
My hands infused into others

The earth is alone
why did the lone river flow into the sea?
lonely the decision.

Aggrieved by those who die
I wake up in the fire
echoing in the stone
Drowning. What tree will grow from the earth?
Call my sorrows a child –
in my hands are broken toys
and before my eyes a man
Countless bodies beg me for eyes
Where shall I let myself begin?

The Heavens are younger than I am
flight has no floor
whose voice can hands be?

Suffer my lies
when you liberate the birds from the forest
Fire tastes the torch
And I dry clothes on the roof of my being
In my distances the eye

میرے لباس میرے دکھ ہیں
میں آگ کا لباس پہننے والی
اپنی چھاؤں کا نام بتاؤں
میں تمام راتوں کے چاند تمہیں دیتی ہوں

سارہ شگفتہ

I am dressed in my sorrows.
Clad in a garment of fire

Shall I tell you the name of my shade?

I give you the moons of all the nights.

+++SARA SHAGUFTA

سمجھوتہ

ملائم گرم سمجھوتے کی چادر
یہ چادر میں نے برسوں میں بنی ہے
کہیں بھی بیچ کے گل بوٹے نہیں ہیں
کسی بھی جھوٹ کا ٹانکا نہیں ہے

اسی میں بھی تن ڈھک لوں گی اپنا
اسی سے تم بھی آسودہ رہو گے!
نہ خوش ہوں گے ، نہ پژمردہ رہیں گے

اسی کو تان کر بن جائے گا گھر
بچھائیں گے تو کھل اٹھے گا آنگن
اٹھائیں گے تو گر جائے گی چلمن

زہرا نگاہ

Compromise

Warm and tendersoft, this *chadur*
Of compromise has taken me years to knit.
No flowers of truth embellish it
Not a single false stitch betrays it.

It will do to cover my body though
And it will bring comfort too,
If not joy, nor sadness to you.

Stretched above us, this will become our home,
Spread beneath us, it will bloom into a garden,
Raise it, and it will become our curtain.

ZEHRA NIGAH

گل چاندنی

گل شام یاد آیا مجھے !
ایسے کہ جیسے خواب تھا
کونے میں آنگن کے مرے
گل چاندنی کا پیڑ تھا

میں ساری ساری دوپہر
سانے میں اس کے کھیلتی
پھولوں کو چھو کر بھاگتی
شاخوں سے مل کر جھولتی
اس کے تنے میں بیسیوں !
لوہے کی کیلیں ٹھنی جڑی
کیلوں کو مت چھونا کبھی
تاکید تھی مجھ کو یہی !
یہ راز مجھ پہ فاش تھا

اس پیڑ پر آسیب تھا !
اک مرد کامل نے مگر
ایسا عمل اس پر کیا
باہر وہ آ سکتا نہیں !!
کیلوں میں اس کو جڑ دیا
ہاں کوئی کیلوں کو اگر
کھینچے گا اوپر کی طرف !
آسیب بھی چھٹ جائے گا
پھولوں کو بھی کھا جائے گا

۱۱۴

The Moonflower Tree

As if in a dream,
I remembered last night,
The tree in a corner of my garden,
Studded with flowers of moonlight.

I would play beneath its shade,
Sheltered afternoons long from the sun,
Swing on the boughs, meeting them as they swayed,
Touch the flowers and run.
Into its trunk had been sunk
Scores of nails.
Many a time had I been warned
Not to touch those nails.

That tree, they said,
Was haunted.
But a wise man
Had cast a spell on it,
Trapped the giant within,
Transfixed him with nails.
Should anyone pull out those pins,
It would release the genie within.

پتوں پہ بھی منڈلائے گا
پھر دیکھتے ہی دیکھتے
یہ گھر کا گھر جل جائے گا
اس صحن جسم و جاں میں بھی
گل چاندنی کا پیڑ ہے !
سب پھول میرے ساتھ ہیں
پتے مرے ہمزاد ہیں
اس پیڑ کا سایہ مجھے !
اب بھی بہت محبوب ہے
اس کے تنے میں ہیں آج تک
آسیب وہ محصور ہے
یہ سوچتی ہوں آج بھی !
کیلوں کو گر چھیڑا کبھی
آسیب بھی چھٹ جائے گا
پتوں سے کیا لینا اسے
پھولوں سے کیا مطلب اسے
بس گھر مرا جل جائے گا
کیا گھر مرا جل جائے گا ؟

زہرا نگاہ

Which would devour every flower,
Which would sap every leaf.
Then this house, this home would burn
In a flash, into ashes it would turn.

Within the confines of this body and soul
Dwells such a moon-silvered tree
Its leaves I've always confided in
Each flower has been a friend to me.
Still, I dearly love
The shade of this, my tree.
And in its trunk until this day
Lives bewitched that same genie.
Even now I live in dread
If ever I should touch those nails
That ogre might escape
The flowers he may not devour
The leaves he may not want
But my home would surely burn!
Would it really into ashes turn?

ZEHRA NIGAH

جرم وعدہ

مرے بچے ہزاروں باریں میں نے تم کو اک قصہ سنایا ہے
کبھی لوری کے آنچل میں
کبھی باتوں کے جھولے میں تمہیں بہلا کے پیٹا کے سلایا ہے
تمہارے گرم رخساروں کو اپنے سرد ہونٹوں سے چھوا ہے
تم سے اک وعدہ کیا ہے
وہی وعدہ • جو انسانوں کی تقدیروں میں لکھا ہے
تحفظ کا • تمہاری آبرو کا • سربلندی کا
مرے بچے
کہانی میں تھکی ہاری جو لڑکی تھی
وہ شہزادی نہیں تھی
وہ جادو کا محل جو ایک پل میں جل کے صحرا ہوگیا تھا • وہ مرا گھر تھا
جہاں آنکھوں کی سوئیاں رہ گئی تھیں
خواب میرے تھے
ہیں جن میں گھر گئی تھی
عزیز کیا سب میرے اپنے تھے
جہاں اس کا فسانہ تھا
وہیں میری حقیقت تھی

My Crime: A Promise

My child I told you a story thousands of times
nestling in the veils of a lullaby
Sometimes I rocked you to sleep, cuddled and cradled
                                          in my words
I touched your warm cheeks with my cold lips
I promised you something
that promise which is the destiny of human beings
of protection, of honour, of esteem.

My child
the tired and exhausted girl in the story
was not a princess, it was me
the enchanted palace
which burnt to a desert in an instant was my home
Where only the needles in the eyes remained*
those dreams were mine
And all those who besieged me
were not outsiders, they were my own kin.
In her story
lies my truth

*refers to the story of a young maiden who has to save a prince by removing thousands of needles pierced into his body by a sorceress. When the last few remain only in his eyes her rival takes over and tricks him into believing that she has saved him.

جہاں وہ مٹر کے پتھر ہو گئی
میری محبت تھی
ہزاروں آگ کے میدان تھے
بارش لو کی تھی
یہ سب کچھ میرا قصہ تھا
یہ سب کچھ مجھ پہ گزری تھی
مرے بچے کہانی میں
تھکی ہاری جو لڑکی تھی
وہ شہزادی نہیں میں تھی

جہاں قصے کا آخر تھا
مرے بچے
وہاں تم تھے
خوشی کی زندگانی کی علامت
تمناؤں کا اک خواب مسلسل
رفاقت کی صداقت کی ضمانت
جہاں پر صرف خوش انجام تھا   ہر ایک افسانہ
مرے بچے ! وہاں تم تھے ، وہاں تم تھے ۔
مری آنکھیں کسی پہچان کے زخموں سے بوجھل تھیں
تمہارا عکس ان زخموں کا مرہم تھا
ادھورے عہد کے رعشے سے میرے ہاتھ لرزاں تھے
تمہارا ساتھ اک تسکین پیہم تھا

۱۲۰

Where she looked back and turned to stone*
there was my love
and thousands of fields of fire
rainfalls of blood
All that was my story
all that happened to me.

My child, in that story
that tired and exhausted girl
was not a princess, it was me.

Where the story ended
my child,
there you came in
a symbol of life and happiness
a constant dream of desires
a guarantee of companionship and truth
where there were only happy endings to every fiction
My child, that's where you came in ... where you came
                                                                                in.

My eyes were weary with the wounds of a promise
Your reflection was a balm to those wounds
My hands trembled with unkept resolutions
your company was a constant comfort

---

* the price of looking back in the story.

مجھے اقرار تھا
میں خاک ہوں
تم حسنِ وزیبائش
مجھے احساس تھا
میں خوف ہوں
تم امن و آسائش
میں مانحی ہوں
مگر تم صورتِ فردا فروزاں ہو
میں مشکل ہوں
مگر تم صورتِ امید آساں ہو۔
مرے بچے
مرا احساس اور اقرار دونوں آج مجرم ہیں
میں اپنا سر جھکائے اپنی فردِ جرم سنتی ہوں
بجانے گل ردائے آرزو سے خار چنتی ہے

تمہیں معلوم ہے
الزام کیا ہے
وہی وعدہ جو النساؤں کی تقدیروں میں لکھا ہے
تحفظ کا ، تمہاری آبرو کا ، سربلندی کا

زہرا نگاہ

I admitted
I am only dust
and you beauty and adornment
I was aware
that I am fear itself
and you peace and comfort
I am the past
but you glow like a future heaven
I am tribulation itself
but you, like hope, are the solution itself

My child
my feelings and admissions both stand guilty today
Head bowed, I listen to the charge against me
Instead of roses I pick thorns from the *chadur* of my
                                                  desires

Do you know
what the allegation is
that promise which is the destiny of human beings
Of protection, of honour, of esteem.

                                        ZEHRA NIGAH

ایک لڑکی

کیسا سخت طوفاں تھا
کتنی تیز بارش تھی
اور میں ایسے موسم میں
جانے کیوں بھٹکتی تھی

وہ سٹرک کے اس جانب
روشنی کے کھمبے سے!
سر لگائے استادہ
آنے والے گاہک کے
انتظار میں گم تھی!
خال و خد کی آرائش
ہو رہی تھی بارش میں
تیر نوک مژگاں کے
مل گئے تھے مٹی میں

گیسووں کی خوش رنگی
اڑ رہی تھی جھونکوں میں
میں نے دل میں یہ سوچا
آب و باد کا ریلا!
اس کو راکھ کر دے گا
یہ سجا بنا چہرہ!
کیا ڈراونا ہو گا
پھر بھی اس کو لے جانا
آنے والے گاہک کا
اپنا حوصلہ ہو گا!

The Girl by the Lamp-Post

A storm raged in the night
the rain poured heavily
on such a night, who knows why,
I wandered aimlessly.
Across the road she stood
against the lamp-post,
her head leaned heavily,
as she waited
for a prospective client.

The make-up ran down her cheeks
in the pouring rain
The arrow-sharpness of eyeliner
was lost in the slush.
The brilliance of her hair
had blown to the winds.
I thought to myself:
this flood of winds and rain
would surely snuff her into ashes,
streak that made-up face
into a ghoulish spectre.
Yet, still, to pick her up,
a prospective client
would need the stomach!

بارشوں نے جب اس کا
رنگ و روپ دھو ڈالا
میں نے ڈرتے ڈرتے پھر
اس کو غور سے دیکھا
سیدھا سادا چہرہ تھا
بھولا بھالا نقشا تھا
رنگ کم سنی جس پر
کیسے دھل کے آیا تھا
زرد پھول سا پتّا
گیسوؤں میں الجھا تھا
شبنمی سا اک قطرہ!
آنکھ پر لرزتا تھا
راکھ کی جگہ اس جا
اک دیا سا جلتا تھا

مجھ کو یوں لگا ایسے!
جیسے میری بیٹی ہو
میری ناز کی پالی
میری کھوکھ جائی ہو
ڈال سے بندھا جھولا
طاق میں سجی گڑیاں
گھریں چھوڑ آئی ہو
تیز تیز چلنے پر
میں نے اس کو ٹوکا ہو

۱۲۴

But when the rain had washed away
those layers of make-up
Once again, fearfully,
I looked at her closely.

A plain, simple face it was,
On those innocent features
surfaced the colours of youth
washed by the rain.
A leaf-like pallid flower
tangled with her hair
A raindrop, like dew,
trembled on her eye.
Instead of ashes, I saw
The glow of a flame.

I felt as if she were
my own daughter
whom I had lovingly raised,
carried in my womb.
A swing dangling from the tree
A shelf laden with dolls I could see
She had left all behind her at home:
I'd gently rebuked her
for walking too fast

ہاتھ تھام لینے پر
میرا اس کا جھگڑا ہو
کھو گئی ہو میلے میں
برگئی ہو ریلے میں
اور پھر اندھیرے میں
اپنے گھر کا دروازہ
خود نہ دیکھ پائی ہو!
دفعتاً یہ دل چاہا
اس کو گود میں بھرلوں
لے کے بھاگ جاؤں میں
ہاتھ جوڑ لوں اس کے
چوم لوں یہ پیشانی!
اور اسے مناؤں میں
پھر سے اپنے آنچل کا
گھونسلا بناؤں میں!
اور اسے چھپاؤں میں

زہرا نگاہ

۱۲۸

She had rebelled
'Gainst her hand being held.

I had lost her then at a fair
Snatched from me by the crowds
And in the darkness
she had not found
the door to her own house.

Suddenly my heart longed
to seize her in my arms
to grab her and run away
to take both her hands
to kiss her brow
to make up with her now.

I longed to turn my veil into a nest,
once again
I longed to shelter her in that nest
once again.

       ZEHRA NIGAH

مری سہیلی

ذہین آنکھیں، کتابی چہرہ، وہ سانولی اک اداس لڑکی!
سفید آنچل سے تن کو ڈھانپے مجھے درچے میں جھانکتی ہے

مری سہیلی وہ ساتھ کھیلی وہ مجھ کو برسوں سے جانتی ہے
وہ دوڑتی ہر کرن کے ہمراہ، میرے گھر میں بلاتی ہے
پھر اپنے ٹھنڈے نحیف ہاتھوں سے میری آنکھوں کو ڈھانپتی ہے
بتاؤ بوجھو کا کھیل ہم دونوں کھیلتے ہیں، وہ ہارتی ہے

ہزار طوفان آئے لیکن یہ دوستی کا گلاب اب تک
ہمارے ذہنوں کے آنگنوں میں اسی طرح سے مہک رہا ہے
ہزار موسم بدل گئے ہیں یہ چاہتوں کا نکھار اب تک
ہماری آنکھوں میں کھل رہا ہے ہمارے رخ پہ دمک رہا ہے
ہمارے اطراف بن دیے ہیں ہزار اندھیروں نے تانے بانے
یہ شعلہ مہر آدمیت اسی روش سے بھڑک رہا ہے،

وہ میرے کمرے میں آکے ہر در کی زیب و زینت کو دیکھتی ہے
وہ ساری الماریوں کے خانوں کو ایک ایک کر کے کھولتی ہے
مری نئی ساڑھیوں کے آنچل وہ اپنے شانے پہ ڈالتی ہے
نئے پرانے تمام گہنے بدن پہ رکھ رکھ کے آنکتی ہے
پھر آئینے کے قریب جا کر وہ بکھری زلفیں سنوارتی ہے
پلٹ کے پھر داد خواہ نظروں کو میرے دل میں اتارتی ہے
میں اس سے کہتی ہوں آؤ بیٹھو، تمہیں زمانے کے رخ دکھاؤں

My Playmate

Bright eyes, oval face, a dark, sad girl
Her body wrapped in a white veil, she peeps through
                              the French windows.
My playmate of many years, she's known me for ages
With the setting rays of the sun she enters.
Her cold, thin hands cover my eyes
We play a guessing game: she loses.

A thousand storms the rose of our friendship has
                                      weathered
Yet still its fragrance blooms in our hearts
A thousand seasons have gone by, still the glow of our
                                      love
Shines liquid in our eyes, radiant on our faces
Though a thousand darknesses cast their sinister nets
                                      around us
Steadfast this flame of human love blazes.

She looks at the decor of the room carefully
Opens every wardrobe to look within
Spreads the sarees across her shoulders to see
Tries the jewellery, both old and new,
then, before the mirror, she arranges her hair
Her gaze, seeking praise, goes straight to my heart.

I say to her, come, sit, I'll teach you the ways of the
                                      world

کہاں کہاں گھوم آئی ہوں میں وہاں کی باتیں تمہیں سناؤں
نئے طریقے تمہیں سمجھاؤں، نئی ادائیں تمہیں سکھاؤں
یہ ساری چیزیں جو دیکھتی ہو میں ان کی بابت تمہیں بتاؤں
یہ ساڑھیاں سب فرانس کی ہیں اور ان کی گلکاریاں بھی دیکھو
یہ ٹیوے سارے اٹالیہ کے ہیں، ساتھ گِر گابیاں بھی دیکھو
یہ نیلی کرنوں میں جھلملاتے، یہ سارے ہیرے ہیں جانتی ہو
یہ موتی مصنوعی حدّ توں کے نہیں ہیں اصلی ہیں مانتی ہو

یہ سچ ہے چیزوں کی اہمیت زندگی میں اک دور مختصر ہے
یہ چھوٹی شیشی کا عطر دنیا میں سب سے مہنگا ہے، کچھ خبر ہے؟
یہ سب خبر خریداری میں نے کی ہے جو سچ کہوں لاجواب کی ہے
ہزار دکانیں دیکھ ڈالیں تو ایک شے انتخاب کی ہے

مگر سنو یہ تمہاری آنکھوں میں کوئی نمی اک چھپی ہے
تم اپنے آنگن سے باہر آؤ، یہ دیکھو دنیا بہت بڑی ہے
وہ نیچی چھت والے دونوں کمروں کے تنگ گھیرے کو توڑ آؤ
وہ گیلی مٹی وہ کونے والا درخت اس کو بھی چھوڑ آؤ
وہ کچی دیوار جس کے سائے میں سب سہانا تھا اسے بھی ڈھا دو
برآمدے کی وہ ٹوٹی چلمن جو ہو سکے کھینچ کر گرا دو!
یہ میری دنیا ہے اس میں آؤ، یہ صاف شفاف دلربا ہے
سہولتیں ہیں حقیقتیں ہیں یہاں پہ ہر رنگ کھل رہا ہے

۱۳۲

Tell you about places where I have been
Let me teach you new ways, let me show you the latest
style
All these things that you see, let me tell you about
them:
All these sarees are from France, just look at the prints
All these bags are from Italy, see the matching shoes?
These sparkling stones are diamonds, did you know
These pearls are real, not artificial, did you know
So true, material goods are a fleeting pleasure
The perfume in this tiny bottle is the most expensive
in the world, did you know
All this merchandise I've bought is matchless, honestly
I shopped in a thousand shops before I made a choice!

But, listen, why are your eyes moist?
Step out of your courtyard, into the huge world
outside
Break out of the narrow bounds of those two, low-
ceilinged rooms
The wet mud, the tree in the corner, leave them
behind
The mud wall which sheltered your agony, knock it
down
Pull down those broken screens in the verandah if you
can
Come into my world, clean, sparkling, seductive
With its comforts and realities every colour glows.

مری سہیلی وہ ساتھ کھیلی وہ میری باتوں کو جانتی ہے
وہ زیرِ لب مسکرا کے آہستگی سے ہر بات مانتی ہے
وہ مجھ سے کہتی ہے آؤ ہم پھر بناؤ بوجھو کا کھیل کھیلیں
تمہارا کہنا ہے اس جہاں میں سہولتیں ہیں حقیقتیں ہیں
حقیقتوں کا وجود کیوں ہے ، سہولتوں کی بنیاد کیا ہے
صداقتوں کے اصول کیا ہیں ، رفاقتوں کا جواز کیا ہے
سہولتوں کی جبیں پہ روشن ہیں میرے آنسو یہ جانتی ہو
حقیقتوں کے لہو میں شامل ہیں خواب میرے یہ مانتی ہو

رفاقتوں کا جواز میرا فراق ، میری جدائیاں ہیں !
صداقتوں کے اصول میری ہی بھولی بسری کہانیاں ہیں !
تمہارے خوابوں کی پاسباں میں ہوں میری یادوں کو تم سنبھالو
جو ہو سکے تو یہ ساری چیزیں جو تم نے دکھلائی ہیں ، اٹھا لو !
وہ ڈوبتی ہر کرن کے ہمراہ میرے گھر میں برا جتی ہے
وہ جاگتی ہر کرن کی سنگت میں اپنے رستے سدھارتی ہے
وہ سانولی ایک اداس لڑکی جو مجھ کو برسوں سے جانتی ہے
یہ کون دیکھے ، یہ کون سمجھے ، وہ جیتتی ہے کہ ہارتی ہے

زہرا نگاہ

۱۳۶

All I have to say my playmate of many years knows
She hides a smile, gently agrees with all I say
Come, she says to me, let's play that guessing game
again.

You say this world offers comforts and realities
What creates those comforts, what makes that reality?
What are the principles of truth, the substance of
friendship?
On the brow of comfort shine my tears, did you know
In the blood of these realities flow my dreams, did you
know
Behind those friendships live my heartaches and
longings.
Those forgotten stories of truth were mine

I am the keeper of your dreams – you keep the
memories that were mine
If you can, take away all these things you have shown
me.

With the setting rays of the sun she comes into my
house
With the waking rays of the sun she finds her way
back
That dark, sad girl who has known me for years

Who can see, who can tell –
Whether she wins or loses?

ZEHRA NIGAH

حدود آرڈیننس

(ان لڑکیوں کے نام جو حدود آرڈیننس کی سزا کاٹ رہی ہیں)

(۱)

میں اک چھوٹے سے کمرے میں
آزاد بھی ہوں اور قید بھی ہوں
اس کمرے میں ایک کھڑکی ہے
جو چھت کے برابر اونچی ہے
جب سورج ڈوبنے لگتا ہے
کمرے کی چھت سے گزرتا ہے
مٹھی بھر کر کرنوں کے زرے
کھڑکی سے اندر آتے ہیں،
اک رستہ سا بن جاتے ہیں

میں اس رستے پر چلتی ہوں
اور اپنے گھر ہو آتی ہوں
میرا باپ ابھی تک میرے لئے
جب شہر سے واپس آتا ہے،
چوڑی کنگھی لے آتا ہے،
آپا میرے حصے کی روٹی،
چنگیر میں ڈھک کر رکھتی ہے

(۲)

پھر چڑیوں کو دے دیتی ہے
میرے دونوں بھائی اب بھی
مسجد میں پڑھنے جاتے ہیں
احکام خداوندی سارے
سنتے ہیں اور دہراتے ہیں

*Hudood Ordinance**

(*To the girls suffering imprisonment under the Hudood Ordinance.*)

In this tiny cell
I am both fettered and free
There's a tiny window
Almost as high as the ceiling
When the sun is about to set
it passes just above it.
A handful of rays
beams through the window
they form a kind of path
for me to tread on
so I can go home.
Even now my father brings me
bangles and combs from the city.
Apa** leaves my share of *rotis****
covered in the bread basket.

2

Then she feeds it to the birds
Both my brothers still go
to the mosque to study
all God's commandments –
they hear and then repeat.

---

*This is an unpublished poem about the Hudood Ordinance, under which some women are still being held. Please see introduction for more details.
**Respectful address for older sister
***Unleavened bread, better known as 'chappatis' in the West.

ماں میرے غم میں پاگل ماں
بس پتھر چنتی رہتی ہے
یا دانہ چگتی چڑیوں سے
کچھ باتیں کرتی رہتی ہے
وہ کہتی ہے جب یہ چڑیاں
سب اس کی بات سمجھ لیں گی
چونچوں میں پتھر چگ لیں گی
پنجوں میں سنگ سمولیں گی
پھر وہ طوفان آ جانے گا
جس سے ہر منصف ہر منبر
پارہ پارہ ہو جائے گا

(۳)

اور میری گواہی وہ دیگا
جو سب کا حاکم اعلیٰ ہے
جو منصف عزت والا ہے

زبر انگاہ

Ma, crazed by her grief for me,
Ma spends her time picking pebbles
or she stays, talking to the birds
as they peck at the birdseed
She says when these birds
understand what she's telling them
they will pick pebbles in their beaks
grasp stones in their claws to hurl
And such a storm shall rage
that every judge and every pulpit
will shatter into smithereens.

3

And He shall be my witness
Who rules the world
Who is both just and gracious.

ZEHRA NIGAH

انتساب

میرا قد
میرے باپ سے اونچا نکلا
اور میری ماں جیت گئی

عشرت آفریں

Dedication

I grew
Taller than my father
And my mother won.

ISHRAT AAFREEN

میں

یہ انا کے قبیلے کی
سفاک لڑکی
تری دسترس سے
بہت دور ہے

عشرت آفریں

I

She belongs to the tribe of Ego*
This ruthless girl
And lives way beyond
The bounds of your territory.

ISHRAT AAFREEN

*Please see notes on Aafreen for an explanation of the term 'ego'.

تعارف

مرا تعارف
پرانے زخموں کو مت کریدو
مرا تعارف
جو تم سمجھتے ہو وہ نہیں ہے
میں اپنی گلیوں کی دھول میں کھیل کر بڑھی ہوں
میں خواب کی عمر میں بپھری حالات سے لڑی ہوں
میں اپنے آبا کی قبر پر کھلنے والی وہ خوش نما کلی ہوں
جو اپنے ہونے کے جرم میں ہر سزا کو ہنس ہنس کر کاٹتی ہے
مرا تعارف تو کچھ نہیں ہے
مرا تعارف تو بس وہی ہے
جو مجھ سے پہلے عظیم غالب کا
میر کا تھا
وہ میر جس کو خدا نے شعر و سخن کا رتبہ عطا ہوا تھا
مگر گدا کی طرح مرا تھا
عظیم غالب
جو مے کی خیرات مانگتا تھا

عشرت آفرین

Introduction

Who am I
Don't scratch old wounds
Who am I
Not what you think I am.
I have grown up playing in the dust of my alleyways
I learnt to fight for myself at an age when others
dream dreams

I am that winsome bud which blooms on my
forefathers' graves
And must smilingly endure every punishment merely
because it exists
I have no name.
Call me by the name
Of the Great Ghalib* who came before me
By the name of Mir
Mir, who was hailed as the god of Poetics and verse
But who died in poverty
The Great Ghalib
Who had to beg for his wine.

ISHRAT AAFREEN

*Ghalib and Mir are both highly esteemed classical poets.

ہجرت

وہ پتھروں کے قبیلے کی بیٹھی لڑکی
روایتوں کی مفیلوں میں خود کو قید کیے
فریب ذات کی اک خوش نما حویلی میں
اکیلے پن کی کتھا سن رہی تھی پھولوں سے
اور اپنے آپ کو بہلا نے تھی پرندوں سے
کہ اس کی روح کی وادی میں اک ہرن جذبہ
قلابچھیں بھرتا ہوا کھائیوں میں دوڑ گیا
یہ پتھروں کے قبیلے کی شہزادی بھی
براعتماد کی زنجیر توڑ کر نکلی
تلاش کرتی ہوئی اپنا وہ ہرن جذبہ
دکھوں کی جھیل کنارے اداس آبیٹھی
وہ خار چبھنے رہی تھی ان کے تلووں سے
کنول ہتھیلیاں چھل کر گلاب ہونے لگیں
شکن شکن تھا خیالوں کا پیرہن سارا
لہو لہو تھا تمناؤں کا بدن سارا
گلابی عمر کے موسم میں گھر سے نکلی تھی
وہ پتھروں کے قبیلے کی ریشمی لڑکی
محبتوں کے قبیلے میں آن پہنچی تھی

عشرت آفرین

Migration

That silken girl from the tribe of Stones
imprisoned herself in the towers of tradition
In a charmed palace of self-deception she sat,
listening to the flowers sing an epic of loneliness.
The birds kept her amused.

Then a gazelle emotion ran into the valley of her soul
Pranced and disappeared into the ravines
This princess of the tribe of Stones, too,
Broke every shackle of trust
And seeking that gazelle emotion sadly came
to rest on the banks of the lake of sorrows
Pulling out thorns from the soles of her ego
Her lotus palms blistered, turned into roses.
Creased
Creased was the robe of her thoughts
Bloody, the body of her desires.

She left home in the pink of her youth
that silken girl from the tribe of Stones
And arrived into the tribe of love.

ISHRAT AAFREEN

ادھورے آدمی سے گفتگو

آخری تجربے نے یہ ثابت کیا
اپنے بھرپور فن، اپنے قامت اور اپنے تشخص کے باوصف
صرف ایک لڑکے ہو تم
جو کہ روتی ہوئی لڑکیوں
یا اڑانوں سے محروم زخمی بدن تتلیوں
ساحلوں سے بندھی کشتیوں
فاختاؤں کے ٹوٹے پروں میں سسکتی ہوئی لذت آزاریوں میں پناہیں تلاشے
جو کھلنڈری سی خواہش کے پیچھے لپکتے ہوئے
اپنے آدرش بھی توڑ دے
میں تمہیں اپنا ادراک و احساس کس طرح دوں
فکر کے اس سفر میں تمہیں کس طرح سائقہ دوں
تم ابھی مجھ سے چھوٹے سے ۔۔۔۔۔ چھوٹے رہو گے
کہ میں اپنے آبا کی ماں ہوں

عشرت آفریں

Dialogue with an Incomplete Man

The final experiment proved:
with all your abundant skills
your stature
and your fine personality
you are merely
a boy, for whom
weeping girls
wounded, wingless butterflies,
boats tied to their anchors
and the sobbing anguish
riding on the broken wings of birds
provide sadistic solace

who, chasing a playful desire,
forfeits his own dignity.

How can I share with you my knowledge and feeling?
How can I take you along on my quest for meaning?

You are still younger than I am
You shall remain younger than I am
I am the mother of my forefathers.

ISHRAT AAFREEN

میرے پرکھوں کی پہلی دعا

رات کی کوکھ سے
صبح کی ایک ننھی کرن نے جنم
یوں لیا
شب نے ننھی شفق کی گلابی، حسیں
مٹھیاں کھول کر
کچھ تکبیریں پڑھیں
اور صبا سے نہ معلوم چپکے سے کیا کہہ دیا
یوں کہ شبنم کی آنکھوں سے آنسو بہے
اک ستارہ ہنسا
چاندنی مسکراتی ہوئی چل پڑی
اور نقاہت سے پہلو بدلتے ہوئے
چونک کر میری ماں نے بڑے شوق سے
کچھ اشارہ کیا
آہٹوں اور سرگوشیوں میں کسی نے کہا
آہ لڑکی ہے یہ؟
اتنی افسردہ آواز میرے خدا
میری پہلی سماعت پہ لکھی گئی
میری پہلی ہی سانسوں میں گھولا گیا
ان شکستہ سے لہجوں کا زہریلا پن
آہ لڑکی ہے
لڑکی ہے
لڑکی ہے یہ !!!

The First Prayer of My Elders

From the womb of the night
A tiny ray of Light was thus born
Night uncurled the lovely pink fists of Dawn
read her palm
whispered to the Morning breeze
and made the dew weep.
A Star laughed
Moonlight smiled and went tripping away

Turning on her side, weakly
my mother started, then keenly
she gestured

A flutter of movement, a whisper:
'Oh! Is it a girl?'

Such deep sadness in that voice, O God!
The very first which wrote itself on to my hearing

In my very first breaths it stirred
the bitter poison of defeat as I heard

'Oh, it's a girl!'
'A girl!'

اس کی قسمت کی مانگوں دعا
ابھی میری سماعت پہ لکھی ہے وہ
میرے پر کھوں کی پہلی دعا

عشرت آفرین

'Is this a girl? Pray for her good fortune, then.'
It is still carved into my hearing
the first prayer of my elders.

> ISHRAT AAFREEN

رہائی

ایسو لوگو اٹھو
اور اٹھ کر پہاڑ کاٹو
پہاڑ مردہ روایتوں کے
پہاڑ اندھی عقیدتوں کے
پہاڑ ظالم عداوتوں کے
ہمارے جسموں کے قید خانوں میں
سینکڑوں بے قرار جسم
اور - - - - اداس روحیں سسک رہی ہیں
وہ زینہ زینہ بھٹک رہی ہیں
ہم ان کو آزاد کب کریں گے
ہمارا ہونا ہماری ان آنے والی نسلوں کے واسطے ہے
ہم ان کے مقروض ہیں
جو ہم سے وجود لیں گے
نمود لیں گے
کٹے ہوئے ایک سر سے لاکھوں سروں کی تخلیق
اب کہانی نہیں رہی ہے
لہو میں جو سنے دھڑک رہی ہے
گمک رہی ہے
ہزاروں آنکھیں
بدن کے خلیوں سے جھانکتی بے قرار آنکھیں
یہ کہہ رہی ہیں

Liberation

Captives
Arise
rise and chisel the mountains
mountains of dead traditions
mountains of blind beliefs
mountains of cruel hatreds.

In the prisons of our bodies
countless restless bodies
and grieving souls sob
they wander round from stairway to stairway
asking us when we shall free them.

Our existence is for the future generations
we owe them,
those who will come into being
through us come into existence.

The severed head which gives birth to thousands
                                          of heads
is no longer just a story.
That which throbs in the blood,
is whining,
thousands of eyes from the veins of the body,
peering restless eyes
are saying this:

اسیر لوگو
جو زرد پتھر کے گھر میں یوں بے حسی کی چادر لپیٹ کر سو رہے ہیں
ان کو کہو
کہ اٹھ کر پہاڑ کاٹیں
ہمیں رہائی کی سوچنا ہے

عشرت آفریں

Captives,
These, who sleep in a house,
of yellow stone
wrapped in sheets of insensitivity
tell them
to rise
and chisel the mountains.
We have to think of liberation.

ISHRAT AAFREEN

غزل

کپاس چنتے ہوئے ہاتھ کتنے پیارے لگے
مجھے زمیں سے محبت کے استعارے لگے

تمام رات جو لڑتے رہے تھے طوفاں سے
عجیب لوگ تھے تھک ہار کر کنارے لگے

مجھے تو باغ بھی مہکا ہوا الاؤ لگا،
مجھے تو پھول بھی ٹھہرے ہوئے شرارے لگے

وہ ہم نہ تھے جسے آنکھیں نچوڑ کر دی تھیں
وہ تم نہ تھے جسے ہم اپنی جان سے پیارے لگے

اس ایک رات قیامت کی بارشیں ٹوٹیں
مری شکستہ حویلی پہ جب پچارے لگے

عشرت آفریں

Ghazal

The hand, picking cotton – I love that hand
A perfect metaphor for the love of the land.

They battled with stormy seas, all night long, and lost
Those strange people, before they reached the land.

Like a fragrant bonfire the garden burned for me
Like stationary sparks the flowers glowed for me.

With eyes wrung dry, that couldn't have been me
Dearer to you than your life, that couldn't have been
me.

That very night such torrents of rain had to pour
When my crumbling home was struck as never before.

ISHRAT AAFREEN

غزل

یہ شہرِ انقلاب کا خوگر نہیں رہا
آئینہ مل گیا ہے تو پتھر نہیں رہا

کس وقت دوستوں نے صلیبیں سجائی ہیں
جب دوش پر کسی کے یہاں سر نہیں رہا

ہم ساحلوں تک آئے تھے حبس کی تلاش میں
پلٹے تو ریت سا بھی وہ ساگر نہیں رہا

اب کس کے لئے ہے سنگ بدستوں کا یہ ہجوم
اس سے کہو کہ شہر میں آذر نہیں رہا

روتی ہیں بستروں میں زمیں منہ لپیٹ کر
ملبوس روشنی کے بدن پر نہیں رہا

عشرت آفرین

١٦٠

Ghazal

This city does not seek a revolution any more
The mirror we found, but the stone we do not have
any more.

At such a time have my comrades found their crosses!
Those who remain have no heads on their shoulders
any more.

In search of the ocean deep we came to the shores
Only to find, even as the sands, the sea was not there
any more.

Why is this crowd still armed with stones?
Aazar* does not live in this city any more.

Weeping, the changing seasons hide their faces in bed
For, on its body, Light does not wear a raiment any
more.

ISHRAT AAFREEN

*Aazar was hounded for sculpting which is forbidden in Islam.

غزل

جنہیں کہ عمر معتبر سہاگ کی دعائیں دی گئیں
سنا ہے اپنی چوڑیاں ہی پیس کر وہ پی گئیں

بہت ہے یہ روایتوں کا زہر ساری عمر کو
جو تلخیاں ہمارے آنچلوں میں باندھ دی گئیں

کبھی نہ ایسی فصل میرے گاؤں میں ہوئی کہ جب
کشم کے بدلے چنریاں گلاب سے رنگی گئیں

وہ جن کے پیرہن کی خوشبوئیں ہوا پہ قرض تھیں
رتوں کی وہ اداس شاہزادیاں چلی گئیں

ان انگلیوں کو چومنا بھی بدعتیں شمار ہو
وہ جن سے خاک پہ نمو کی آیتیں لکھی گئیں

سروں کا یہ لگان اب کے فصل کون لے گیا
یہ کس کی کھیتیاں تھیں اور کس کو سونپ دی گئیں

عشرت آفریں

Ghazal

All their lives long prayers for marital bliss they heard
Yet they crushed their own glass bangles, to drink I heard.*

Enough poison there is of traditions to last us a lifetime
From sorrows they gave us knotted inside our veils.

Never was there a harvest in my village,
When the rose, not the *kussum*, should have dyed our veils.

To the fragrances of their apparel the wind owed a debt
Those sad princesses of all seasons who have now left.

Even kissing those fingers is a sin, I reckon,
Which inscribe on dust the verses of creation.

Who stole the levies on the harvest this year to keep?
Who owns these fields, and look, who got them to keep?

ISHRAT AAFREEN

*Suicide – traditionally upheld as a virtuous way out of a bad marriage.

غزل

اب کی برکھا کیاری کیاری جگنو بوئے جائیں گے
دہقانوں کی بیواؤں کے آنسو بوئے جائیں گے

کب تک سرداروں کی حویلی لے گی خون کسانوں کا
کب تک اس کی بنیادوں میں گھڑ و بوئے جائیں گے

جانے کس کی ڈھیٹ لگی ہے میری سبز زمینوں کو
گاڑے جائیں گے تعویز اور جادو بوئے جائیں گے

جب تک مٹی کی زرخیزی پہ سننے والے زندہ ہیں
اپنے خون کی بوندیں میرے گبرو بوئے جائیں گے

ذہنوں ذہنوں خوابوں، پھول کھلانے والے ہاتھ
رنگ دھنک، چاند اور سرگم کی خوشبو بوئے جائیں گے

عشرت آفریں

Ghazal

Come the rains this year, in every flower bed fireflies
                                      shall be planted
The tears of the widows of peasants shall be planted.

How long will the *havelis** of the landlords bleed the
                                        peasants?
How long will rosy cheeks in their foundations be
                                        planted?

Heaven knows whose voodoo has struck my green
                                        fields
Charms will be dug in and magic shall be planted.

So long as those who suck the fertile soil dry still live,
My youths shall let the drops of their own blood be
                                        planted.

Hands that make flowers bloom from mind to mind
                                      and dream to dream
Rainbow colours, the moon, the fragrance of the
                                      notes of music shall be planted.

ISHRAT AAFREEN

*The distinctive, affluent home of the feudal landlord

غزل

یہ نازک سی مرے اندر کی لڑکی
عجب جذبے عجب تیور کی لڑکی

یونہی زخمی نہیں ہیں ہاتھ میرے
تراشی میں نے اک پتھر کی لڑکی

کھڑی ہے فکر کے آذر کدے میں
بریدہ دست پھر آذر کی لڑکی

انا کھوئی تو کٹ کٹ کر مر گئی
بڑی حساس تھی اندر کی لڑکی

سزاوار ہنر مجھ کو نہ ٹھہرا
یہ فن میرا نہیں آخر کی لڑکی

بکھر کر شیشہ شیشہ ریزہ ریزہ
سمٹ کر پھول سے پیکر کی لڑکی

حویلی کے کہیں تو چاہتے تھے
کہ گھر ہی میں رہے یہ گھر کی لڑکی

عشرت آفرین

۱۶۶

Ghazal

Hidden inside me lives this delicate girl
Strange aspect, strange passions she has, this girl.

    I can tell you why my hands bleed so:
    Bare hands chiselled her from stone, this girl.

Again in the pagan temple of thought she stands
With her wounded hands – she must be Aazar's* girl.

    She died of grief, when they stole her dignity
    So tender was the girl who lived inside this girl.

Why should you blame me for this art?
I am not the artist, nor am I Aazar's girl.

Though she scatters into myriad crystals
She curls into the apparition of a flower, this girl.

The owners of the *haveli*** really wanted
To keep within the family their own girl.***

ISHRAT AAFREEN

*See note on p. 161
**See note on the previous page
***reference to arranging marriages within the family to conserve capital

غزل

بھوک کی کڑوواہٹ سے سرد کسیلے ہونٹ
خون اگلتے ، سوکھے ، پھٹنے ، پیلے ہونٹ

ٹوٹی چوڑی ، ٹھنڈی لڑکی ، باسی عمر
سبز بدن ، پتھرائی آنکھیں ، نیلے ہونٹ

سونا آنگن ، تنہا عورت ، لمبی عمر
خالی آنکھیں ، بھیگا آنچل ، گیلے ہونٹ

کچے پکے لفظوں کا یہ نیلا زہر
چھو جائے تو مورکھ کو بھی چھیلے ہونٹ

زہر ہی مانگیں امرت رس کو منہ نہ لگائیں
باسی ، ضدی ، وحشی اور ہٹیلے ہونٹ

ایسی بنجر باتیں ایسے کڑوے بول
ایسے سندر کومل سرخ رسیلے ہونٹ

اتنا بولو گی تو کیا سوچیں گے لوگ
رسم یہاں کی یہ ہے ، لڑکی سی لے ہونٹ

عشرت آفرین

Ghazal

The bitter taste of hunger on cold lips
Blood-spitting, cracked, dry, yellow lips.

Broken bangle, icy girl, rebellious age
Green body, stony eyes, and blue lips.

Bare courtyard, lone woman, long years
Blank eyes, damp veil, moist lips.

Blue poison from bitter words grazes
Peels off these peeling lips.

Begging for poison, refusing honey dew
Rebellious, stubborn, wild, wilful lips.

Derelict thoughts, bitter words
Lovely, gentle, red, juicy lips.

What will they say to all this talk:
'Girls, they say, must seal their lips.'

ISHRAT AAFREEN

غزل

لڑکیاں ماؤں جیسے مقدر کیوں رکھتی ہیں
تن صحرا اور آنکھ سمندر کیوں رکھتی ہیں

عورتیں اپنے دکھ کی وراثت کس کو دیں گی
صندوقوں میں بند یہ زیور کیوں رکھتی ہیں

وہ جو آپ ہی پوجی جانے کے لائق تھیں
چھپا سی پلوروں میں پتھر کیوں رکھتی ہیں

وہ جو رہی ہیں خالی پیٹ اور ننگے پاؤں
بچا بچا کر سر کی چادر کیوں رکھتی ہیں

بند حویلی میں جو سانحے ہو جاتے ہیں
ان کی خبر دیواریں اکثر کیوں رکھتی ہیں

صبحِ وصال کی کرنیں ہم سے پلو چھپا رہی ہیں
راتیں اپنے ہاتھ میں خنجر کیوں رکھتی ہیں

عشرت آفریں

Ghazal

Why do girls follow the destinies of their mothers?
Why are their bodies deserts, their eyes the ocean deep?

Why do women keep their jewels locked in trunks
To whom will they bequeath their legacy of grief?

Those who were themselves worthy of worship
Why do they clutch stones between jasmine fingertips?

Those who remained hungry and barefooted
Why do they never let their *chadurs* slip?

When tragedies strike behind a closed door
Why do the walls often seem to know?

Shining upon our union ask the rays of the morning sun
Why are the nights armed with daggers when they come?

ISHRAT AAFREEN

بنتِ زر

حویلی میں مقید
سورما کی لاڈلی بیٹی
تھکن سے چور
نا آسودگی سے مضمحل
موسم کی شکوہ سنج
بے حد زود رنج
فضایں بارشوں سے قبل کی گہری گھٹن
اور حبس کا عالم
اسی عالم میں وہ لڑکی
دریچوں سے
سنہری ، ریشمیں پردوں کو سرکا کر
عجب حیرت سے
ان کھیتوں کی جانب رخ کئے
چپ چاپ بیٹھی ہے
جہاں پر لڑکیاں
کلکاریاں بھرتی ہوئی
پائل کو جھنکارتی
گلابی اور دھانی چیزیاں اوڑھے ہوئے
پھرتی ہیں اٹھلاتی
کہ جن کے پاوؑں میں محنت نے گھنگھرو باندھ رکھے ہیں
کہ جن کے ہاتھ میں ہر بٹہ ہے مٹی سے محبت کا
نشہ ہے جن کی آنکھوں میں فقط گندم کی حدت کا

۱۷۲

The Daughter of Riches

Imprisoned in the *haveli**
the stalwart's darling daughter
crushed with fatigue,
drained by dissatisfaction,
laments the weather
feeling very tetchy.

Laden with the deep oppressiveness
waiting for the rain,
the atmosphere feels close.

Feeling suffocated, the girl
moves the golden silky curtains
a fraction
from the French windows
with a strange wistfulness.
Sits quietly
With her face towards the fields
where the girls
chattering
clinking their anklets,
wearing pink and light green scarves
walk around with a swagger.
For around their feet diligence has tied anklets
for in their hands is the harp of love for the soil
for in their eyes is the intoxication merely of the
                                  warmth of wheat.

* See footnote on p. 165.

وہ بنتِ زر
نہایت رشک سے
ان بے بضاعت
کم لباس
اور کم غذا چہروں کو تکتی ہے
کہ جن میں زندگی کی ایک سچی لو دمکتی ہے

عشرت آفریں

That daughter of riches
with great envy
watches these landless
poorly dressed
poorly fed faces
in which glows the true fire of life.

        ISHRAT AAFREEN

بارہ فروری ۱۹۸۳ء

(۱۲ فروری ۱۹۸۳ء کو لاہور کی خواتین نے قانونِ شہادت کے خلاف ایک جلوس نکالا جس پر پولیس نے تشدد کیا ۔ یہ نظم اس واقعہ کے بعد لکھی گئی)

سنو مریم ، سنو خدیجہ ، سنو فاطمہ
سال نو کی خوشخبری سنو
اب والدین بچیوں کے جنم پہ
انہیں موت کے ٹیکے لگوائیں گے
کہ
قانون اور اختیارات ان ہاتھوں میں ہے
جو پھول ، علم اور آزادی کے خلاف
لکھتے ہیں ، بولتے ہیں ، فیصلہ سناتے ہیں
حاکم اور ثقہ مانے جاتے ہیں
ہاں سنو مریم ، سنو خدیجہ ، سنو فاطمہ !
آج وہ ایسا قانون بناتے ہیں
کہ آنکھوں سے لگاؤ
ہونٹوں سے چومو
احسان مانو اور شکرانہ ادا کرو ۔
گھر کی ملکہ ہو
بچوں کی ماں ہو
سر جھکا کے خدمت کرتی کتنی اچھی لگتی ہو
کیسی محفوظ اور پروقار ہو
بلند مقام اور جنت کی حقدار ہو ۔
اس لیے تمہارے بھلے کو بتاتے ہیں
" دو عورتوں کی گواہی " سمجھاتے ہیں ۔
یوں تنہا نکلنا ٹھیک نہیں
آنا جانا مناسب نہیں
یہ حکم آسمانی ہے

*Twelfth of February, 1983**

Hear me Maryam, hear me Khadija, hear me Fatima
Hear the good news of the new year
on the birth of their daughters
parents will now seek deadly injections for them
for law and power is in the hands of those
who write, speak out and adjudicate against
flowers, knowledge and freedom.
They govern, they are the rulers.

Yes, hear me Maryam, hear me Khadija, hear me Fatima
Today they make laws
which you must touch with your eyes
kiss with your lips
for which you must be grateful, thankful.
You are the queen of your home
mother of your children
head bent in servitude, how lovely you look
how protected and dignified
you have a right to a pedestal and Heaven
therefore, they tell you for your own good
want you to understand 'the evidence of two women'.*

Going out alone is not right
all these comings and goings are improper
this is a heavenly injunction

*Please see introduction

جسے ماننا نجات کی نشانی ہے
جو اس سے انکاری ہے
ارتداد کا مجرم
قابل گردن زدنی ہے
سڑکوں پر نکلنا
لڑنا بھڑنا
آزادی کا حق مانگنا
نسوانی تقدس کے خلاف ہے
غنڈوں کا کام ہے
کیوں اس نازک وجود کو تھکاتی ہو
ہلکان کرتی ہو
چینی کی گڑیا ہو
نظروں میں آؤ گی
ٹوٹ کے بکھر جاؤ گی
تیز دھوپ میں پگھل جاؤ گی
عدالت میں سچی بات کہہ نہ پاؤ گی
شرم و حیا سے چپ ہو جاؤ گی
لاج کی ماری بے ہوش ہو جاؤ گی
ماتمی جھنڈیاں پھر پھڑپھڑا رہی تھیں
کنیزیں باغی ہو گئی تھیں
وہ دو سو عورتیں
چاروں طرف سے گھری ہوئی تھیں
مسلح پولیس کے نرغے میں تھیں
آنسو گیس، رائفل اور بندوقیں
وائرلیس دین اور جیپیں
ہر راستے کی ناکہ بندی تھی
کوئی پناہ نہ تھی
یہ لڑائی خود ہی لڑنی تھی

whoever denies this
is guilty of apostasy
deserves to be beheaded.*

To come out on the streets
to fight
to demand the right for freedom
is against the sanctity of the feminine principle
is the work of ruffians.
Why do you tire this delicate body,
exhaust it?
You're a china doll
you'll get noticed
get smashed, get shattered to pieces
you'll melt in the hot sun,
you won't be able to tell the truth in court
modesty and shame will make you silent
you'll faint with embarrassment.

The flags of mourning were flapping
the handmaidens had rebelled
Those two hundred women who came out on
                                 the streets
were surrounded on all sides
besieged by armed police.
Tear gas, rifles and guns
wireless vans and jeeps
every path was blockaded
there was no protection
they had to fight themselves.

*Another fundamentalist demand

179

وہ پالتو اور پچھیتے
جمیعت کے غنڈے
جب سڑکوں پر دندناتے تھے
آگ لگاتے لوٹ مار کرتے تھے
بر چھے بھالے لگماتے تھے
شہریوں کو دھمکاتے تھے
تب یہ آہنی ٹوپی والے
دور سے دیکھ کر مسکراتے تھے
شفقت سے ہنستے تھے
بچے ہیں ۔۔۔۔۔۔۔۔۔۔۔
کہہ کر دودھ پلاتے تھے ۔
عورت کا پیچھا چھوڑ و
اور اپنی فکر کرو
یہ کھو کھلے اخلاقی بندشن اور ضابطے
اپنی حکمرانی کے واسطے
مجھے کیوں سمجھاتے ہو ؟
کیا اسلام لانا اتنا مشکل ہے
کیا اب سے پہلے لوگ نماز نہ پڑھتے تھے
کیا روزہ نہ رکھتے تھے
یا قرآن اور کلمے کو نہ مانتے تھے ؟
پھر کیوں جوانیوں کو برباد کرتے ہو
اتنے کمضور اور ظالم بنتے ہو
بات بات پہ کوڑے مارتے ہو

۱۸۰

Those pets and favourites
the hoodlums of the Jamiat*
when they raved along the streets
set fires and looted
swung spears and shields
terrorised the citizens
then these helmet-wearers
smiled from a distance
laughed affectionately
'They're only kids . . .'
they said, and fed them milk.

Let women be
Watch your own interests.
These hollow moral rules and restraints
for your own power
why do you explain these to me?
Is Islam that difficult?
Did people never pray before now
did they not fast?
Did they not believe in the Quran and the
                                      Kalima?**

---

*The leading Islamic party which collaborated with the army
**The basic tenet of faith affirming the Unity of God and Mohammad's prophethood.

اذیبت پہنچاتے ہو ۔
میں آزادی کا منشور پڑھ چکی ہوں
اور تم !
لکھا ہوا جو سامنے ہے
اتنا موٹا اور واضح ہے
نوشتۂ دیوار ہے
پڑھنے سے قاصر ہو ۔
یہ تم نے کیسے سمجھا ؟
کہ تم کو پیدا کرتی ہوں
اور عتبارے سامنے شرما کر ، لجا کر
سچ کہنے سے گھبراؤں گی
زبان سے وہ سب ادا نہ کر پاؤں گی
جو ہم دونوں کے بیچ
محبت ، نفرت ، عزت اور حقارت کا رشتہ ہے
کیا عورت کی سچائی سے ڈرتے ہو ؟
کیا میں ماؤف ہوں ؟
یا ذہن میرا مفلوج ہے
کہ ساتھ کھڑی میری ہم جنس
مجھے یاد کراتی رہے
مجھے تو رتی رتی یاد ہے
تمہیں بھی یاد کرانا جانتی ہوں
یاد کرو............کہ ظلم
قانون کے حوالے سے خوب پہچانا جاتا ہے

۱۸۲

Then why do you destroy youth?
Why be so cruel and relentless?
Why use the whip for every little thing
and torture?

I read the charter of freedom
And you?
The writing in front of us
is large and clear
written on the wall –
are you unable to read?

How did you think this?
I who give birth to you
would be too shy and embarrassed before you
would worry about speaking the truth
won't be able to describe with my tongue
that relationship between the two of us
of love and hatred, of respect and contempt.

Are you afraid of a woman's truth?
Am I numb?
Or is my mind so paralysed
that standing next to me another person of my sex
should remind me?
I remember every detail
I want to remind you
Remember . . . that cruelty
can be identified with reference to the law
can be understood.

سمجھ میں آتا ہے
تم مجھ سے انسان کا درجہ چھینتے ہو
میں تمہیں جنم دینے سے انکار کرتی ہوں
کیا میرے جسم کا مصرف یہی ہے
کہ پیٹ میں بچہ پلتا رہے
تمہارے لئے اندھے ، بہرے ، گونگے
غلاموں کی فوج تیار کرتی رہے
ہم جانتے ہیں کہ تمہارا ساتھ دے کر
ہم اپنے بچوں کی قبریں کھودیں گے
اس لئے ہم تمہارا ساتھ نہیں دیں گے ۔
تم دو کہتے ہو
ہم دو کروڑ عورتیں
اس ظلم اور جبر کے خلاف
گواہی دیں گے
جو قانون شہادت کے نام پر
تم نے ہمارے سروں پہ مارا ہے
ہم نہیں تم
واجب القتل ہو
کہ روشنی اور سچائی کے دشمن ہو
محبت کے قاتل ہو ۔

سعیدہ غزدار

۱۸۴

You snatch from me the status of a human being
I refuse to give birth to you
Is this the only use of my body
that my womb should nurture a child
raise for you an army of slaves
blind, deaf and mute?
We know that if we support you
we shall be digging the graves of our children
so we shall not support you.

You ask for two
We two *crores** of women
shall testify
against this tyranny and cruelty
hurled at our heads
in the name of the law of evidence

Not us, but you
deserve to be murdered
for being the enemies of light and truth
for being the murderers of love.

SAEEDA GAZDAR

*Equals ten million.

چور

میرے تن پر بھوک آئی تھی
میری آنکھیں منگی تھی
اور میرے آنگن میں ہر جا
غربت ، بھوک اور محرومی کے
پھول اُگے تھے
میرے کانٹے ہاتھوں نے
ان پھولوں کو توڑنا چاہا
اور ہمسایے کے گھر سے
جس کے گھر میں
سونے، چاندی اور پیسوں کی
دیواریں تھیں
اپنے لئے کچھ خوشیاں چن لیں
چور ، چور ، چور ، چور
کچھ آوازیں
پھر زنجیریں
پھر میرے ہی گھر کی مانند
بدبو دار اندھیرا کمرہ
جس کے باہر
مجھ جیسے بے چہرہ لوگ
میرے لئے پہرے پہ کھڑے تھے

نیلما سرور

The Thief

Hunger grew on my body
my eyes were bare
and everywhere in my back garden
poverty, hunger and deprivation
were in bloom.

My thorny fingers
tried to pluck those flowers
and from the neighbours' houses
in which
stood walls
of gold, silver and coins
plucked some happiness for myself.

A thief! A thief! A thief! A thief!
some voices
then chains
then a house somewhat like my own
a smelly dark room
outside which
some faceless people
like myself
stood guard around me.

                                    NEELMA SARWAR

حوالات

پھولوں والے باغ میں بیٹھ کر
ایک بڑا سا پنجرہ دیکھا
جس میں کچھ انسان بھرے تھے
پیلی رنگت
وحشی آنکھیں
بکھرے بالوں والے انسان

چھوٹے سے اس تنگ پنجرے میں
کچھ بیٹھے تھے ۔ کچھ لیٹے تھے
لیکن سب کچھ سوچ رہے تھے
شاید اپنی اپنی سزائیں
یا پھر اپنے اپنے جرائم
یا ان لوگوں کے بارے میں
جو پنجرے سے باہر بیٹھے
آزادی پر نازاں تھے

نیلما سرور

Prison

As I sat in a garden full of flowers
I saw a huge cage
crammed with human beings,
pallid of hue
wild-eyed
wild-haired human beings
in that small cramped cage.

Some sat, some lay on the floor
but they were all thinking something.

Perhaps of their punishments
or of their crimes
or, maybe, about those people
who sat outside the cage
and smugly presumed they were free.

NEELMA SARWAR

کوڑوں کی سزا پانیوالے پہلے شخص کے نام

تو میرے دور کا عیسیٰ ہے
جس نے قوم کے سارے گناہ ہوں
ساری برائیوں، ساری سزاؤں
کو اپنے کندھے پر اٹھا کر کوڑے کھائے
ہم سب چور ہیں
ہم سب زانی
ہم سب رشوت خور لیڈرے
پھر سب کے حصے کی سزا
تم نے کیوں پائی؟
اور ہم چاروں اور کھڑے
تیرا تماشا دیکھ رہے تھے
جیسے تم نے جرم کیا تھا
اور ہم سارے پارسا تھے

نیلما سرور

To the First Man to Be Awarded Lashes

You are the Messiah of my times
who, bearing all the sins of the nation,
all the evils, all the punishment,
on your shoulders received the lashes.

We are all thieves
We are all fornicators
We are all corrupt robbers
Then, the punishment which everyone deserved
Why did *you* receive it?

And we stood on all four sides
watching this spectacle
as if you had committed the crime
and we were all virtuous.

NEELMA SARWAR

کاش وہ روز حشر بھی آئے

تو میرے ہمراہ کھڑا ہو
ساری دنیا پتھر لے کر
جب مجھ کو سنگسار کرے
تو اپنی باہنوں میں چھپا کر
پھر بھی مجھ سے پیار کرے

نیلما سرور

I Wish That Day of Judgment Would Come

... When you would be beside me.

Armed with bricks, when the whole world
stones me to death –
then you, hiding me in your arms,
would carry on loving me still.

NEELMA SARWAR